Cyberliteracy

Cyber

NAVIGATING THE INTERNE

literacy

WITH AWARENESS

Laura J. Gurak

Yale University Press New Haven & London

Set in New Baskerville and Officina type by The Composing Room of Michigan, Inc.

Printed in the United States of America by R. R. Donnelley & Sons.

Library of Congress Cataloging-in-Publication Data
Gurak, Laura J.
Cyberliteracy : navigating the Internet with awareness / Laura J. Gurak.
   p.   cm.
Includes bibliographical references and index.
ISBN 0-300-08979-1
1. Internet literacy.   I. Title.
TK5105.875.I57 G88   2001
004.67′8 — DC21   2001017972

A catalogue record for this book is available from the British Library.

The paper in this book meets the guidelines for permanence and durability of the
Committee on Production Guidelines for Book Longevity of the Council on Library
Resources.

10 9 8 7 6 5 4 3 2 1

Contents

ACKNOWLEDGMENTS

Like the Internet, books, even those that purport to be written by a single author, are in the end collaborative—linked, hypertextual documents that stand on the shoulders not so much of giants than of the many individual inspirations, discussions, and nexus points that take place among students, friends, and colleagues. So many times, it is during or after a great conversation—face-to-face or over the Internet—that one suddenly realizes just how to explain an issue or characterize a topic. If each of us could create links from our own words to the inspirations we gain from others, the resulting documents would be far more unwieldy than any of today's Web sites. The best we can do is to use a good system of citations and thank those who do not fall into that category. Herein, my thanks.

I thank the University of Minnesota, particularly the College of Agricultural, Food, and Environmental Sciences, as well as the Department of Rhetoric, for its support of projects that are not only academic but also attempt to bring research and scholarly criticism to the public. In addition, I wish to thank the many fine students I have had, particularly those students in my Internet Studies seminars. Thanks also to my colleagues for their good cheer and support. And many thanks to my colleague Mary Lay, who, upon hearing me sketch out the idea for this book, said those fatal words: "You'd better write it before someone else does."

Many of the chapters contained herein are based on commentaries I gave on the radio show "Future Tense: A Journal of the Digital Age" (Minnesota Public Radio). I thank "Future Tense" founder and producer Jon Gordon for teaching me a few things about writing for broad, non-academic audiences and for giving me the chance to bring my ideas to the public radio audience.

Works to which I owe gratitude are Sherry Turkle's *Life on the Screen* and Stephen Doheny-Farina's *The Wired Neighborhood*. Both books take a close look at social issues in cyberspace and weave in scholarly commentary while remaining accessible to a wide audience. In addition, early research in computer-mediated communication set the stage, more than ten years ago, for social and cultural criticism of cyberspace, and I am grateful for being able to build on these insights. Susan Herring's work on gender and online communication has been central to most discussions, and David Kaufer and Kathleen Carley's axioms of communication provide a basis for my notions of speed and reach. Kathleen Welch's work on electric rhetoric also provides a framework in which to orient my analysis; I am particularly grateful for her support and enthusiasm about this project.

My thanks to Lenna Constantinides for her assistance with the final stages of this project, and to Jonathan Cihlar, Jenni Swenson, and Wendy Winn for their work with the Internet Studies Center. Thanks also to Chris Silker for her help with locating Web sites. And I thank my sister Carol Felts for her editorial assistance throughout.

Thanks also to Dan Burk of the University of Minnesota Law School for his discussions about legal issues and to Julie Cohen of Georgetown University Law Center for her thoughts about fair use and the Web.

I am grateful to Rolf Norgaard of the University of Colorado at Boulder, Jack Selzer of Pennsylvania State University, Barbara Warnick of the University of Washington, John G. Norman of Ohio State University, and one anonymous reviewer, all of whom provided excellent feedback on the early versions of this project. I should also like to express my most sincere appreciation to Jean Thomson Black, my editor at Yale University Press, for her support, encouragement, vision, and superb editorial approach on this project. I am also grateful to Jenya Weinreb of Yale University Press for her careful and thoughtful copyediting.

Finally, I thank my partner and intellectual companion, Nancy Bayer, for her continuous support and encouragement of this and all my various projects.

Cyberliteracy

In late December 2000, a man (MM for short) who worked as a quality assurance tester brought a bag of weapons to work and opened fire on his co-workers at a Massachusetts-based Internet startup firm, killing seven people and rocketing the United States back to a waking state after the consumer-induced hype of the winter holiday season. In initial news reports, people said the things we are by now sadly used to hearing after these sort of shootings: "He seemed OK, sort of quiet, kept to himself." But within days, reporters at *Wired* magazine had discovered what they claimed was MM's digital side by checking out his cyberspace identity, tracing all they could find based on an email address presumably belonging to MM (based on the name, city, and other similarities). We suddenly knew that his Amazon.com wish list included movies like *Lethal Weapon* and *Die Hard with a Vengeance* and that he posted notes to the Usenet newsgroup alt.engr.explosives. We knew his email address and his digital description of himself. And when the *New York Times* covered this online side of the story on 8 January 2001, it included the Web address, or URL, of MM's Amazon wish list. If you thought that the Internet was nothing more than an interactive version of television, think again.

Welcome to the information age, circa 2001, where nothing is quite like it used to be and everything is the same, only more so.

When the Internet first came into being, it was designed so that people could share information across a non-hierarchical structure. And that was well and good when those people were researchers and academics. No one could have foreseen the clash between this unwieldy system, created with the equally unstructured UNIX operating system, and the most structured forces on the planet: corporations, news agencies, and others who thrive on information. Now we have robots scouring Web sites, matching up your data with your shopping habits, following your mouse clicks to see where you go and what you like. Just on the horizon: refrigerators and other kitchen appliances that know what you want for breakfast. Soon people will take for granted the ability to check out someone's criminal record over the Internet or track down an address or phone number without leaving their chairs.

Other features of life in cyberspace are changing some of our most basic assumptions. What we used to separate into "speech" and "writing" is now blending together; notice how the text of most email messages actually sounds like spoken language and is often sloppy, with little concern for spelling, capitalization, formality. American English is changing, and as these words migrate into other cultures, so too are other languages. Uppercase and lowercase letters are now blended in ways that still can't be checked with a spell checker or style guide: eBay, netLibrary, ican, amazon.com, and so on. Notions of who owns what and what you can and cannot use without permission (also called copyright) are changing, too. We tell students not to plagiarize, but they continue to cut and paste from Web pages to homework assignments and to create sites that let you download entire term papers. All too often, even the most skeptical among us accept a piece of online information without having a clue as to where that information came from or who wrote it.

To most people, technologies are not about choices. Technologies are invented, advertised, packaged up, and sold to you. Technologies do not have backgrounds or politics, and technologies do not, in and of themselves, make you do things. In a talk I gave as part of a seminar on ecommerce in early 2001, an audience member challenged me, believing that technologies themselves are neutral and that it's how we humans use these technologies that requires our attention. That may be true. But technologies are invented by people and imbued with design choices that give these devices (software included) certain trajectories. What if today's email systems were designed not to promote individual values but group ones; for example, what if every time you wanted to post an email message, it needed a second signature from someone else in your organization or community? Not only does today's Internet allow individual postings, it allows anonymous ones, too. The choices built into the Internet, and the choices we then make about how to use it, require a far more critical framework than we currently have.

Enter cyberliteracy: a set of concepts and critical views with which to understand today's Internet. This book, a result of years of observation, research, and experience, arises from a previous project, one where I first noticed that issues of privacy, electronic information, and the Internet were going to be problematic for years to come. In the early to mid-1990s, two online protests shook the still nascent place called cyberspace. The first, the protest over Lotus MarketPlace, was possibly the first case of social action on the Internet. When privacy advocates and others heard about the product (a CD-ROM that contained demographics and spending information), they rebelled, using email and Usenet newsgroups to protest. A few years later, when the Clinton administration announced an encryption standard called the Clipper chip, advocates again took to the digital airwaves to create one of the first online petitions.

Since my research on these controversies (published as *Persuasion and Privacy in Cyberspace* in 1997), I have continued to observe the Internet and its phenomenal growth and change. The protest over MarketPlace seems minor now, because much of the same demographic information is available via numerous Web sites. And the concept of encryption, foreign to most of us in 1994, is now familiar to anyone who shops over the Internet. We have come to accept as givens much of what these early protests were about: the use and sale of personal information, for example, are reaching fever pitch on ecommerce sites and created, for a time, the most inflated series of stocks that the market has seen. Despite surveys showing that personal privacy is a major concern for most Internet users, high-level policy makers show little interest in stopping the wholesale collection and sale of personal information on the Internet. The ubiquity of the Internet has brought with it an acceptance of certain social conditions that are linked to the technology.

The Internet's intense growth has continued to spark my interest in understanding the social side of cyberspace. Changes to our social spaces, our use of language, and our political and economic realities are ever more complex as the Internet becomes the mass communication medium of a new era. I am not alone in my desire to understand the human side of this technology. Numerous scholars and critics have joined the effort to help users understand cyberspace in all its complexities. But unlike some academic studies, social and critical perspectives of life online are of interest to a broad audience. For example, I am often interviewed by local and national media to discuss life in cyberspace as we enter the twenty-first century. Although it's common for academics to comment publicly about their research, what seems unusual in my case is the broad range of people who want my opinion and the regularity with which they consult me. University researchers and administrators, journalists, radio reporters, policy analysts, government officials, secondary education teachers, technical writers, technology managers, and executives—these are just some of the professionals who have contacted me over the past five years seeking words of wisdom about what Sherry Turkle has accurately called "life on the screen." I am an occasional commentator for Minnesota Public Radio, featured on local and national television, and called on to provide material for newspaper or magazine articles.

Several issues strike me each time I talk with people outside my profession. First, I've realized how important it is to capture the critical issues of online communication in a nutshell, skipping past jargon and getting to the heart of the issues that matter to people. Second, people usually have the same questions or comments. The answers are familiar to me (because I know the research literature and have been an Internet scholar for more than a decade), but not to them (because this literature is specialized and spread across many disciplines). In other words, what seems like commonplace information to me is new and exciting for others. Finally, and perhaps most important, it's become apparent to me that what everyone is *really* concerned with (although they don't say so explicitly) is a new *literacy*—specifically, a new literacy for the new media. This desire is expressed in the sorts of questions people are asking: How is communication accomplished online? What are appropriate strategies for persuasion, negotiation, or corporate communication? How are gender and identity perceived online? Why do rumors and hoaxes seem to flourish in this environment? How do I, a private citizen, or we, a corporation, deal with this form of communication? It is against this cultural backdrop that I write this book.

What I offer is a book of broad appeal, organized around topics that are and will continue to be central when it comes to participating in life on the Internet. In this sense, this book is something of a rubric or a guide to literacy in cyberspace: a guide to cyberliteracy.

Unlike many of the "how-to" books and "dummies' guides" on the market, this book is not a technical listing of what to do and not do. Its topics are not connected with any particular technology, software version, or computer system but are more general to the nexus between social issues and the Internet. Concerns about privacy and technology, for example, will not go away simply because of new encryption technology or new self-regulatory moves on the part of industry. In fact, recent trends suggest that privacy could become an even greater concern in the coming years. Similarly, issues about rumors online or gender in cyberspace will continue to be important, even as Web browsers change and modem speeds increase. These are *social* issues, not just technical ones, and they are at the heart of what I believe should constitute our thinking about any new kind of literacy we propose for the coming years.

This book remains tied to the research studies that inform its topics. These studies, some of which date back to the 1980s, have proved themselves general enough to withstand shifts in technology. For example, early research on hierarchies and email continues to be relevant, even though email technology has changed vastly from the days when this work was done. Studies of gender online are also based in broader theory—theory that I believe will hold up even as the Internet evolves and grows. So, while this book is not overtly theoretical, it is based on certain long-standing work in technology studies. Each chapter centers on my own observations and case examples taken from the Internet, print media, and other sources that I have been collecting for several years.

Readers may notice that many of my examples are from sites that offer Minnesota themes. I have tried to use these regional examples as a way of maintaining some balance between the wide world of cyberspace and my own, local community in Minnesota, a theme I discuss in the final chapter.

I am trained as a rhetorician, which is to say as a scholar of language with a particular interest in how symbols, including language, sound, and visual communication, are used as persuading and motivating forces. Accordingly, this book takes a rhetorical approach to its subject. It examines the motivations—via language, images, sounds, and screen—behind the newly emerging technologies of digital communication. Whereas *Persuasion and Privacy* took an overtly rhetorical stance, invoking classical concepts from rhetorical theory (delivery, ethos, kairos), this book takes a more subtle approach. It uses a form of rhetorical analysis often categorized as "eclectic." (Scholars and others who are interested in my approach can find more information in the Appendix.) This approach involves examining key terms and concepts in order to learn about the motives behind a technology. In selecting the terms that I find to be critical for cyberliteracy, I am inviting the reader to experience, understand, and view the digital world through my lens and my interpretation. Like any critic, I acknowledge that there are many other ways to interpret these artifacts. I invite readers to continue the discussion and challenge my interpretation.

This style of criticism, it strikes me, is very much in keeping with the pace and structure of communication online: if you don't agree, post a note and start a new discussion. It's indeed eclectic and hypertextual, but in the end, there is strength in drawing from a range of critical perspectives. It is similar to the strengths one can find when drawing from the vast well of commentary and criticism posted to any Web site or Usenet newsgroup.

The key concepts that I have chosen for this book—speed, reach, identity, privacy, and so on—are apparent in the mainstream discourse surrounding the Internet and all its varied features. Newspapers, magazines, television newscasts, shows on public television: all these markings of popular culture tell us that the Internet cannot be ignored. In my encounters with students, their parents, journalists, friends, audiences at keynote addresses, and so on, I have noted that there are certain elements about the Internet that they, the people who use the technology, want to understand. And they want to understand these elements in ways that go far beyond what they are offered by those who are selling the technologies. While the mainstream discussion today may emphasize ecommerce, the broader landscape includes people wondering about all the social, workplace, and educational issues surrounding the Internet: community, home and work lives, identity, computers and anger, myths and hoaxes, and so on.

Yet we tend to examine these issues only in the most cursory fashion. If you don't like having information about you spread throughout the Internet, you're told just to turn off the "cookies" in your browser. If you have questions about how having different screen identities may affect people's behavior at work, you're chided for being a Luddite and not being part of this "wave of the future." And if you get angry when you keep receiving junk-mail email messages, the company that sent them will tell you that you can always delete them. Our culture does not inspire us to look beyond these simplistic answers to understand the broader social issues that these questions raise. Nor are we inspired to protest or change the technology. Yet to be cyberliterate means to recognize that technologies have consequences, and that we can decide how we allow the Internet to be part of our lives.

In addition, research, writing, and activism on issues of copyright and cyberspace have been crucial in keeping our awareness attuned to how technology affects policy. When Congress proposed to extend the term of copyright by yet another 25 years (making the term the life of the author plus 75 years) and proposed another bill that would have made simply downloading a Web page a copyright infringement, scholar-activists came together to fight these bills under an umbrella group called the Digital Futures Coalition. Humanists and legal scholars alike, including Andrea Lunsford, Dennis Karjala, John Logie, Karen Lefevre, Martha Woodmansee, Peter Jaszi, and many others took a stand on these issues, invoking the sort of active cyberliteracy that this book proposes. In the end, the term of copyright was extended, but this does not mean we should abandon our desire to take action on issues involving Internet technology and our lives.

This book is written for people who use the Internet and understand some of the underlying rhetorical and social elements of this technology. You can read it from cover to cover, or you can use it to focus on a particular topic. Chapters 1 and 2 explain the concept of cyberliteracy and the key terms that are used throughout the book. Each of the remaining chapters focuses on a particular topic. If you are interested in privacy but not gender, for example, you can go directly to the appropriate chapter. In a way, the book is designed in a hypertextual fashion, like a Web site. Chapters 1 and 2 are the main Web page, and the other chapters are links that you can read in any order you like. A section titled "Sites for Cyberliteracy" includes additional links for more information; readers can also visit the companion Web site at www.cyberliteracy.net. The Appendix explains my theoretical and methodological choices as well as my choices about obtaining permission to reprint the illustrations in this book.

In the end, technologies are what we make them. Hardware and software do not follow some predetermined path toward a predetermined future. As a result, we must take a critical, informed stance about the Internet in order to be cyberliterate. Otherwise, we go blindly into a new communications era unprepared to understand and engage the ways the Internet, and all its future iterations, is enmeshed in the fabric of our daily lives.

There's no turning back. Once a novelty, the Internet is now transforming how Americans live, think, talk, and love; how we go to school, make money, see the doctor, and elect presidents. This isn't just about the future — it's about the here and now.
—*Newsweek* (20 September 1999, 39)

By "literacy" I mean . . . not only the ability to read and write but an activity of the minds . . . capable of recognizing and engaging substantive issues along with the ways that minds, sensibilities, and emotions are constructed by and within communities whose members communicate through specific technologies. In other words, literacy has to do with consciousness: how we know what we know and a recognition of the historical, ideological and technological forces that inevitably operate in all human beings.
—Kathleen Welch (1999, 67)

Fifty years ago, the above quotation from *Newsweek* would have been impossible to comprehend. As an early, pre-Web Internet user, I for one could not have imagined this technology becoming so common that the obscure UNIX term for the period, "dot," would be a word used in daily conversation. Yet today, many of us live in a state constantly mediated between our physical lives and our electronic ones, moving between our physical spaces (homes, classrooms, and offices) and our private e-spaces (voice-mail boxes, email, and chat sites) without thinking much about it. We do this even though this way of living is radically different from what most humans have experienced until now. More and more, we do it to the tune of what big corporations see as the Internet's future. And we do it, almost always, with little critical observation of our own behavior. We're too busy moving along the superhighway, the metaphor that brought us to this place, to stop and ask how much we like it, how it affects our physical lives, and whether the current Internet offers the best model for the long-term good of society.

Yet if we stepped back not so long ago in the United States, or if we dropped in today to a country more rooted in its villages, neighborhoods, and localities, we would experience a completely different sense of things. We would become aware of how slowly life moved and how long it took to eat a meal, bake bread, shop for clothing, or read a book. I suspect that many of us would long to return to our hyper-paced life, to the early part of the twenty-first century in the United States where the global blended with the local, the physical with the virtual, the human with the machine. I know that part of me would be unhappy living in a slower, less wired time. But I am not completely pleased with how our wired lives are turning out. The efficiency of the Internet is great, and the ability to reach out to others and tap into vast sources of information and ideas, generated by anyone from a sixth-grader to a major news organization, is profound. Yet more and more of the Internet is being used to make money, gather our personal information, protect corporate intellectual property, and encourage us to shop. In addition, the ways we now think about our social spaces are changing dramatically in response to how these technologies are being implemented. We expect to send and receive email with incredible speed and get angry if replies don't come quickly enough. When it comes to email, we care less and less about spelling or grammar. We sit at individual screens, staring into the flicker, waiting for our virtual friends to appear, while our other friends and family sit in the next room. How we view the world and how we live in it are being shaped by the features of these new technologies.

Scholars have thought about these issues for some time now. Yet as cybertechnologies—the Web, email, voice mail, interactive television, and new technologies to come—become cheaper, easier to access, and more ubiquitous, questions that once mattered only to specialists studying online communication are now on the minds of almost every person who conducts business, pursues hobbies, enlists political support, finds a date, or keeps in touch with distant friends and family in our wired, edgy, postmodern world. Open up any newspaper or magazine, and you are sure to find an article or two about the social side of the Internet. People seem aware that this technology has profound implications for them, but they also have many questions; for example, the special issue of *Newsweek* quoted in the epigraph raises questions about business, medicine, politics, and education in the wired age.

In this book I argue that in terms of current discussion—at home, in the classroom, and in the boardroom—what we really need to understand is not just how to use the technology but how to live with it, participate in it, and take control of it. In other words, what we need is a new literacy, a critical literacy, for this new medium. Unless people become familiar with the social, rhetorical, and political features of digital communication, they will be led into cyberspace with only a limited understanding of both the power and the problems of this technology. To become cyberliterate, people need to understand the topics addressed in this book, not only to become more efficient computer users but also to become more sophisticated about critiquing, challenging, and anticipating how these technologies are designed, implemented, and used.

Survey after survey shows that Internet users are at once excited and nervous about the potentials of this new technology. The issue of online privacy illustrates this point. In a survey conducted by the Annenberg Public Policy Center at the University of Pennsylvania (1999), 70 percent of parents with computers felt that the Internet offered children opportunities for learning. But even more parents (75 percent) were concerned about how these new technologies might be used to gather personal information or provide access to unacceptable images and text. So while parents want children to use the Internet, these same parents fear problems they do not understand and cannot control. Privacy is in fact a key concern regarding today's Internet. Yet with few public forums available for this sort of discussion, and with congressional debates led mostly by business interests that favor little or no regulation of data privacy, the proverbial "man on the street" (updated to "person on the wires") feels that he or she has few choices about online technologies and privacy. Cyberliteracy, taught at all educational levels and incorporated into how we approach this technology, would cause Internet users to question the privacy issue: to reject sites that don't have clear privacy policies and to lobby their representatives for more comprehensive approaches to privacy and technology.

By inviting readers to use the Internet critically, this book offers a set of tools for navigating the new terrain. It asks readers to be active participants in cyberspace and to become familiar with both the obvious and the not-so-obvious features. It suggests that to be truly literate online, users must understand the economic and political forces that are shaping information technologies. For technologies are not neutral. They do not develop in isolation from the social, political, and (most important in the United States) economic powers. Cyberliteracy involves, as Welch suggests in the second epigraph to this chapter, a *conscious* interaction with the new technologies: one that embraces and enjoys the technology but at the same time is critical, looking beyond the enticing Web images or speedier data connections that dominate our images of cyberspace.

Defining Literacy and Cyberliteracy

What is cyberliteracy? The term *literacy* is a highly contested one; I will provide a brief overview of this issue to illustrate how I am using the concept. Looking at this overview leads one to the logical conclusion that in the digital age, the concept of literacy must be reconfigured if it is to be useful for helping us understand communication in the future.

Kathleen Tyner, in *Literacy in a Digital World* (1998), provides a succinct overview of the literacy debate. She notes that in general, the term *literacy* is often equated with the ability to read and write. Before World War II, scholars wrote about "literacy as a tool for transforming higher psychological processes" (25). This ideological perspective—that being able to read and write was somehow transformative and brought people to a "higher level" of cognitive ability—valued certain types of ability over others; thus, scholars were making vast judgments about the superiority of one culture over another. Western cultures, living in the post-Gutenberg world of print, were, according to this way of thinking, superior to many traditional, indigenous cultures that communicated their history and cultural knowledge orally (through stories, poetry, song, and so on). As studies of human society became more culturally sensitive, this older view of literacy was hotly contested, and people realized that what "counts" as literacy in one culture may not be the same in another.[1] In a more open view, all forms of discourse from all cultures are also forms of literacy.

And yet, popular understandings of literacy often hearken back to those more biased, simplistic definitions, valuing reading and print over any other form of communication. This view of literacy is what might be labeled as "performative": that is, the ability to do something is what counts. We hear about literacy in this way almost every day when we watch the television news or read the paper and learn that people need to become more "computer literate" or "technology literate," which, translated, usually means that these people need to learn how to use a computer and keyboard. Indeed, this view of literacy is so common that it leaves little room for what I am suggesting: a critical technological literacy, one that includes performance but also relies heavily on people's ability to understand, criticize, and make judgments about a technology's interactions with, and effects on, culture.

In addition to literacy as performance, most people understand literacy to mean "print," and thus we have come to favor the book over the screen. As Welch, Tyner, and others have argued, print dominance has profound implications for higher education, because while students spend hours watching television and playing on the computer, their schoolwork still focuses on printed books.

One way to update this print-limited view of literacy to include electronic texts is to consider the work of Walter Ong. Ong's notion of "secondary orality" helps describe the language we use on the Internet (email, Usenet news, the Web)—language that is a blend of written and spoken communication.

I would be remiss to discuss Ong's work without noting its critics. Some people believe that Ong's analysis of oral and print cultures is biased, suggesting the inevitability of print and the superiority of those who live in the Gutenberg world, and they often draw on the following passage to make their case: "Oral cultures indeed produce powerful and beautiful verbal performances of high artistic and human worth, which are no longer even possible once writing has taken possession of the psyche. Nevertheless, without writing, human consciousness cannot achieve its fuller potentials, cannot produce other beautiful and powerful creations. In this sense, orality needs to produce and is destined to produce writing" (Ong 1988, 14–15). For this sort of thinking, Ong has taken his share of criticism, because these words may be interpreted to favor the white, European, post-Gutenberg world of print over numerous other oral traditions—traditions that are equally powerful and significant. He has, however, since modified his position.[2]

Ong's concept of secondary orality helps us consider cyberliteracy because it illustrates that electronic communication is in fact different from speech and different from print. A simple analysis of almost any email message illustrates this point. According to Ong, secondary orality combines features of print culture with features of oral culture. Like print, email is typed. It is fixed in a medium, for however long, and like a printed book can be distributed widely.[3] Yet email texts sound more liked typed conversations than printed material. (Spelling and capitalization are often ignored, for example.)

Ong identifies nine features of oral discourse, noting in one example that oral style is "additive rather than subordinative" (37); that is, each sentence builds on the previous one using certain parts of speech and rhythm. Others of Ong's oral characteristics— aggregative rather than analytical; redundant; conservative; close to the human lifeworld; agonistically toned; empathetic and participatory; homeostatic; situational—are useful in seeing how the "written" e-texts of electronic discussions (like email) resemble both writing and speech (Figure 1.1).[4]

This analysis helps us see that cyberliteracy is not purely a print literacy, nor is it purely an oral literacy. It is an electronic literacy— newly emerging in a new medium—that combines features of both print and the spoken word, and it does so in ways that change how we read, speak, think, and interact with others. Once we see that online texts are not exactly written *or* spoken, we begin to understand that cyberliteracy requires a special form of critical thinking. Com-

Get Msg New Msg Reply Reply All Forward File Next Print Delete Stop

Folder Name | Subject | To/From | Date | Priority

Local Mail
- Inbox
- Unse...ages
- Drafts
- Templates
- Sent
- Trash
- ATT...000
- Dept. stuff

Undeliverable mail | Postmaster@minds.c... | 12:29 PM
Re: Fwd: FW: l   open house | l   k | 12:47 PM
undergrad admissions requireme... | Laura J. Gurak, Ph.D. | 12:56 PM
Re: ATTW 2000 Conference Prop... l | | 1:01 PM
FYI | Nancy Bayer | 1:01 PM

Subject: Re: Fwd: FW: L   open house
Date: Tue, 2 Nov 1999 11:47:46 -0600
From: L   K   l
To: gurakl@tc.umn.edu
References: 1, 2

Sounds good. I'm sorry the dates collided!

l-a

>OK. I'll let Jay know. Maybe you can I could go over some time and do a
>brown bag presentation to the people at   about our respective
>research and we could also get a tour.
>
>LG
>
>
>J   wrote:
>>
>> Yes, you're right, it would not be a good idea to reschedule the DGS
>> meeting. And as much as I would like to stay at T'   for the tour, I
>> really don't want to miss another DGS meeting. I've already missed one.
>> Whether or not we get to my DGS item next week, I'd still like to be there.
>> I'll plan on going there for lunch, but perhaps I could visit   for a
>> more extended tour some other time.
>>
>>

771 messages, 2 unread

Figure 1.1. A typical email message contains features of both writing and speech, illustrating Ong's notion of secondary orality and, more broadly, the idea that cyberliteracy requires reading and listening skills not usually accounted for in print. Notice that although this, like all email messages, is laid out like a memo (Subject, Date, From, To), the tone is more like oral communication: short, incomplete sentences, lowercase letters, informal signatures ("l-a"). The format is also "aggregative" in that each locution builds on the previous one. *Source:* Laura Gurak.

munication in the online world is not quite like anything else. Written messages, such as letters (even when written on a computer), are usually created slowly and with reflection, allowing the writer to think and revise even as the document is chugging away at the printer. But electronic discourse encourages us to reply quickly, often in a more oral style: we blur the normally accepted distinctions (such as writing versus speaking) and conventions (such as punctuation and spelling). Normal rules about writing, editing, and revising a document do not make much sense in this environment. So it is not adequate simply to assume a performative literacy stance and think that if we teach people to use computers, they will become "literate." Cyberliteracy (again noting Welch) is about *consciousness*. It is about taking a critical perspective on a technology that is radically transforming the world.

A Review of Western Literacy Technologies

To be cyberliterate means that we need to understand the relationship between our communication technologies and ourselves, our communities, and our cultures. It may be hard to see the effects of the Internet and cyberspace on our daily lives, in large part because we are living in the midst of these changes. Already we take so much for granted. Email messages containing photos of your family in another state; real-time chats and instant messages; Web sites for almost every product, service, and idea imaginable — these features have quickly become part of our daily landscape. And even as these technologies shift into different shapes (new versions of software, faster Internet connections), they continue to affect how we view the world. Tyner's observation is astute: "Some literacy technologies atrophy from widespread disuse, but the conventions they foster in form and content may linger for centuries" (1998, 40). Cutting and pasting, kerning, the standard size of a page ($8^1/_2 \times 11$ inches) — all these ideas come from an older print technology but have made their way into new technologies like word processing and Web page design.

Many people have become familiar with the standard litany of communication technologies in Western history: most books about the Internet have sections that describe the printing press, telegraph, radio, telephone, television, and so on. Each particular narrative paints a story to the author's liking, but most suggest in some way or another that these technologies led us to where we are today. The idea that today's Internet is a direct descendent of Gutenberg was canonized when the Arts and Entertainment cable channel, in October 1999, named the thirteenth-century inventor and craftsman the "#1 person in the millennium" (after a long countdown of the "top 100"). Yet what is often missing from these popularized accounts is a look at the relationship between communication technologies, cultures, and worldviews. Many scholars (Walter Ong, Elizabeth Eisenstein, and Arnold Pacey—to name just a few) have observed these relationships between our tools and our times. In order to gain perspective on cyberliteracy, it is useful to revisit the history of communication technologies and look at how these technologies have altered cultures.[5]

In the Western story of literacy and technology, we often begin by looking at the stone counting devices used by ancient peoples to keep track of commerce, such as the sale of domesticated animals or grain (Faigley 1999). These technologies created what David Kaufer and Kathleen Carley (1993) call a "technological situation . . . a set of available [communication] technologies and their distribution across individuals in the society" (99). Along with word of mouth and memory, farmers and tradespeople could rely on these inscribed pieces of clay to remind them who owed them a sheep or some wheat or barley. This technology increased the "reach" (see Chapter 2) of communication, because individuals did not need to be near each other to have a record of their transaction. A similar discussion takes place around the papyrus scroll; Aristotle's manuscripts were the length that they were in part because they needed to fit the size of a standard scroll (Aristotle 1991, 13). Social conditions changed, as Plato's oft-quoted *Phaedrus* dialogue tells us, when people began to record oral discourse onto these paper scrolls. And when the Catholic Church controlled manuscripts, another set of social conditions emerged: knowledge was in the hands of the priests and monks who maintained and copied these documents. As movable type and the Gutenberg printing press caught on, everyday people could own a Bible or a novel. Books and pamphlets, and issues of who could print and own them, became the subjects of many political battles, but in the end, the book—particularly the paperback—became what some would call a profound communication technology.[6] It is small and lightweight. It does not require batteries. You can read it and pass it along to someone else. Indeed, from stone etchings to paperback novels, the shapes we have given the technologies of reading and writing have in turn become the shapes of how we live with each other.

Next in this narrative come electronic technologies, which speeded up the transmission of information, increased the number of people who received this information (see Chapter 2), and began to move information from tangible ink on the page to electrified characters and sounds sent over wires. The impact of the telegraph and train, telephone, radio, and television has been studied widely by media critics, social historians, and historians and critics of technology. In fact, the telegraph brought with it changes very similar to those we see with the Internet: Tom Standage, in *The Victorian Internet* (1998), calls the telegraph the "mother of all networks" and describes how this technology hinted at what we now find so profound about Internet communication: speed, reach, online romance, news and media coverage, and "a technological subculture with its own customs and vocabulary" (viii).

Every communication technology, based on the choices made when it was designed and developed, changed our senses of space, community, and self. Each technology changed our sense of what we expect from our friends and our political leaders: until recently, for example, politicians needed to travel by plane or train to make personal connections with their constituencies. Later it was possible to use radio and television, but citizens were not able to talk back to these one-way technologies. Today politicians can stay in touch via the Web, and citizens fully expect to be able to do so; Governor Jesse Ventura of Minnesota, for example, has maintained a successful Web site both before and after his election (Figure 1.2).

People born in the midst of a new technology, before it becomes ubiquitous, are often keenly aware of these social and cultural changes (never more so than today, when commentary about the Internet is everywhere). Many of us who are now over 40 learned to write first with paper and pencil, then with a typewriter. We adapted our writing styles and techniques as each iteration of word processor came along, from the dedicated machines of the 1980s (like the Wang) to the more intuitive software of Word Perfect and Microsoft Word. Despite great strides in user interfaces, screen resolutions, and processing speeds, many people—particularly in my age group—have trouble editing on screen. At a certain stage, we need to print out our memo, essay, or letter because of what researcher

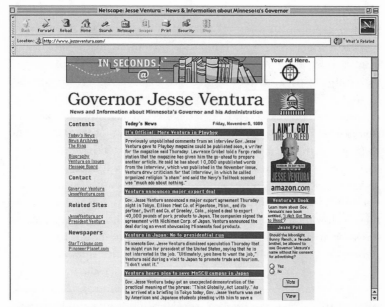

Figure 1.2. Unlike most other political Web sites, which often are no more than digitized magazine pages, Governor Jesse Ventura's interactive Web site played a major role in getting out his message during his campaign. Even now that he has been elected, the governor maintains an interesting, interactive site.
Source: www.jesseventura.com.

Christina Haas (1996) has characterized as the "text sense problem." The people she studied indicated that when they used the computer to write, they had "a hard time *knowing where [they were]*" (120) and often felt disconnected and lost in the screen text.

Many of us who teach writing have noticed that a younger generation, surrounded by screens and buttons, are comfortable with writing, editing, and navigating completely within the digital text. They live in a world of digitized space. Before they could even speak, they watched people channel surf, press buttons to heat things in a microwave, and navigate the Web. This generation does not always create a document with the goal of printing it (a feature of early word processing); what they produce on the screen often *is* the final product (a Web page, for example). Our technologies condition

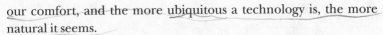

our comfort, and the more ubiquitous a technology is, the more natural it seems.

Discussions of electronic technologies often focus on how we read and write in this space. Perhaps because writing instructors were some of the first to be confronted with computers in the classroom, a wide body of commentary and research has developed to consider this particular feature of e-technologies: how we work with text affects how we read and write.[7] Linear ways of thinking go by the wayside the more one begins to be surrounded by chunks of information, sound bites, and "site bites" (Welch 1999).

Yet the relationship between our communication technologies and our lives is not only a cognitive one. It is a political one as well. New technologies are often used to reinforce, not change, current power structures. On the Internet, this phenomenon is readily apparent. Take Marshall McLuhan's concept of the "global village." Paul Levinson (1999) notes the aptness of this concept, originally conceived with television in mind, for today's Internet: "The advent of computer screens not only as receivers but initiators of information in homes and offices around the world . . . [fulfills] another of McLuhan's observations about the global village—namely, that its dispersion of information is creating a new power structure whose 'centers are everywhere and margins are nowhere'" (7). But even though the Internet inspires new global models, many of the best grassroots sites are being bought out and sold on the traditional stock market. They now have CEOs, worry about profit margins, and are subject to large mergers (like AOL and Time Warner).

Another example is copyright, which should be opening up in light of the ability to share via the Internet. Instead, copyright is getting even more restrictive: U.S. legislation passed in 1998 (the so-called Sonny Bono Copyright Extension Act) was favored by powerful publishing and entertainment lobbies and extended the term of copyright by another 20 years. Most proposed legislation continues to favor copyright holders and not the public.

Cyberliteracy, then, takes into account many features. For years, educators have talked about a critical literacy in the context of students using printed books. Cyberliteracy electrifies the discussion, inviting us now, while the technology is growing all around us, to consider what is different about Internet communication. Cyberliteracy recognizes that on the Internet, communication is a blend of oral, written, and visual information: the technology, like many before it, shapes our social spaces, replacing the slower methods of handwriting and typing with the speed and frenzy of digitized text. The Internet has broad reach like television, but it is interactive like a conversation. While inviting a "global village," the technology is embedded in a political and economic context of corporate mergers and government regulations.

Literacy as a Value System

There is one more feature to take into account. In some cases, the term *literacy* not only means performance and written language, it also indicates exactly what one *should* read and write. E. D. Hirsch's book *Cultural Literacy* (1988) is often cited as the paradigm case. Hirsch's canon of what counts as knowledge has been widely criticized for some of the same reasons as accounts that value print over oral literacy. Canons are always problematic, because what they include will always privilege some people's stories, plays, art, or ideas over others. Welch's (1999) definition of literacy at the end of the millennium reminds us that, as with all attempts to define what counts as literacy, cyberliteracy is not neutral in value. Drawing on her own analysis and the work of literacy theorist Brian Street (1984), she argues that literacy in an age of electric rhetoric must make room for differing kinds of knowledge and must recognize that literacy is always connected to issues of power—who owns information and who controls it. She notes that literacy "constitutes intersubjective activity in encoding and decoding screen and alphabetic texts within specific cultural practices and recognizes the inevitable deployment of power and the control that larger entities have over these media. . . . While literacy now and historically is conditioned by communication technology, it is not determined by it; changes in consciousness bring about social constructions in which some writing and speaking activities are privileged and others are devalued" (136).

Because the most common definitions of electronic literacy con-

centrate on the performative aspects, they often ignore this important lesson. When people of European descent forced Native Americans to give up their languages and stories and adopt the languages
and stories of the Western world, they were taking an overtly biased
stance in defining what counts. Likewise, we must be careful that
definitions of computer literacy do not favor some groups over others. Online communication, which bears the marks of both speech
and writing, has the potential for restoring orality to an inherently
Western print-oriented world, and it provides new opportunities for
determining what kinds of information are considered valid.

Yet these potentialities will not become actualities unless people
who are traditionally underrepresented in the computer culture
(African Americans, Native Americans, women) are welcomed into
the world of computing. Even though Internet use is increasing, not
everyone has access. According to a Commerce Department study
on the "digital divide," more than 40 percent of households in the
United States owned computers in 1999, but only 25 percent had
Internet access. Furthermore, the report notes, "the bright picture
is clouded by data that show significant disparities continue between certain demographic groups and regions and, in many cases,
the gap between these groups has grown over time" (U.S. Commerce 1999). In fact, not everyone has access to even the basic infrastructure. In a different study, the National Telecommunications
Information Administration reported that high percentages of the
Native American population do not even have phone service (Anderson 1999).

Access problems are not limited to the United States. Freeman
Dyson (1999) notes that in order for all the world's citizens to benefit from the global economy via the Internet, access must be made
available to individual homes and families, regardless of location.
He admits, however, that political and economic realities make such
an ideal difficult to implement.

To end this discussion of access, it is important to return for a moment to the most basic concept of literacy: the ability to read and
write. Even if people have computers, they will not be able to access
the great potential of online technology if they cannot understand
printed text. Yet in a 1999 study by the Literacy Volunteers of Amer-

ica, 21–23 percent of those studied were unable to fill out an employment application, follow written instructions, or read a newspaper.

This question of access is important. For the Internet to realize its potential, cyberspaces of the future must represent the range of human experience rather than just corporations, media conglomerates, and the predominantly white, male world of engineering and computing, which until now has been the main force in coding and developing the Internet (see Chapter 4). The Internet should be accessible to all via hardware and phone access and via online spaces that are open to a range of cultural perspectives. Individuals and groups representing diverse cultures, viewpoints, and ideas should stake out their claims in cyberspace before it is too late.

A Challenge to Technological Determinism

For most citizens, it is hard to imagine that the course of any technological development might have been different. That is because we are raised on a model of technological development based on the theory of evolution. Historian and critic David F. Noble best describes this mythos in his case study of factory automation, where he argues:

> It is a staple of current thinking about technological change that such a "successful" technology, having become dominant, must have evolved in some "necessary" way. Implicit in the modern ideology of technological progress is the belief that the process of technological development is analogous to that of natural selection. It is thus assumed that all technological alternatives are always considered, that they are disinterestedly evaluated on their technical merits, and that they are then judged according to the cold calculus of accumulation. Any successful technology, therefore—one which becomes the dominant and ultimately the only solution to a given problem—must, by definition, be the best, for it alone has survived the rigors of engineering experimentation and the trials of the competitive marketplace. And, as the best, it has become the latest, and necessary, step along the unilinear path of progress. (Noble 1986, 144)

Noble easily could have been describing the Internet, which is constantly being hyped in the press and among the populace in overtly Darwinian terms.[8] Examples abound; in a *New York Times* article discussing Microsoft's corporate strategy, we hear that "Microsoft Corporation conceded today that the company now [faces] an even greater challenge in the next phase of the Internet's *evolution*, as the role of traditional desktop software recedes and the power center of computing shifts from the operating system to the World Wide Web" (Lohr 1999; emphasis added).

This short sentence is rife with unspoken but key premises. The writer's use of "evolution," for example, suggests that there is a single pre-defined path for how the Internet will develop. The desktop will recede, and the Web will become the center of operations. Although this scenario is certainly possible and has some advantages (software would always be updated, for example), it is not the only option. Operating systems will probably still be important features of personal computing. Not all applications will or should run via the Web: no matter how well a page or database is encrypted, consumers may prefer to keep their checking-account information on their hard drive, not on a Web site.

Unlike what this example suggests, the Web is not a biological entity that will somehow evolve on its own.[9] In fact, Microsoft is one of the key players in determining how personal computing and the Internet will develop. If Microsoft, with all its power and control, were to decide that the operating system should still be the "power center" of computing, it is hard to imagine that this would not happen. In this sentence, however, Microsoft is set up as a neutral observer, watching the "evolution" of this thing called the Internet and speculating on how the company could keep up with the forces of natural selection. Yet Microsoft is hardly neutral; it is one of the biggest forces in technology development today.

Technological Darwinism suggests that the power of the consumer is equivalent to the forces of natural selection, and that if a product is faulty, it will drop off the evolutionary tree simply because people do not purchase it. But major forces—Internet companies, the telecommunications and cable industry, entertainment and media conglomerates, and government officials (who make laws based mostly on what they learn from lobbyists)—are making overt choices about what the Internet will be and do. Remember Betamax, the video standard that was developed around the same time as VHS? Many people felt that Betamax was actually the higher-quality product of the two. But VHS became the default standard, not because it was better or even because consumers preferred it, but because of intense marketing efforts and Sony's decision to discontinue the Betamax technology.

Other visions about the Internet never make it to market, not because they fail the test of economic evolution but because they are not supported by the powers-that-be. In the early days of the Internet, just before the hubbub of Web shopping mania and overpriced stock offerings, many people were speculating about the role the Internet could play in democratic discourse, education, and public information. But with legislators favoring a laissez-faire policy toward the Internet and at the same time reducing any remaining federal government funding, the Internet quickly turned into a predominantly commercial space. One is reminded of cable television in the 1970s, which some people hoped would reinvigorate democracy and give citizens access to television's power and reach but which has since become a wasteland of commercials and commercial stations. Alternate possibilities will seem less and less likely unless we invoke an activist stance, becoming energized citizens of cyberspace who challenge determinism in our research, in what we teach, and in the technologies we favor.

Moving beyond Ecommerce

Commercial forces on the Internet are not completely bad. Competition leads to new ideas and often makes products cheaper and more available to consumers. Computer hardware prices have dropped dramatically in the past three years. Newer and better Web sites and search engines are available. And new business models, inspired by the Internet's people-driven, bottom-up style, are changing how we do business. Yet there is cause for concern when we take a medium with such potential and let it develop entirely within a laissez-faire model. Especially in today's climate, this model ignores issues of social good, public space, and citizen access.

Cyberliteracy invites us to look beyond the commercial and see that this is a technology about communication, not just selling. It is a technology of reading, writing, and speaking, and it brings with it changes in everything affected by human communication, from grammar and style to conceptions of community, expectations about speed, differing senses of gender and identity, new ways to think about hate speech and censorship, and new ways to conduct politics. And a cyberliterate look at the Internet also reminds us that in the end, we must still learn to live with each other in the physical world.

I am not alone in this quest. Several groups, including Computer Professionals for Social Responsibility (CPSR) and People for Internet Responsibility (PFIR) share the idea that cyberspace should be more than online shopping malls. PFIR (1999) notes that "with the rapid commercialization of the Internet and its World Wide Web during the 1990's, there are increasing concerns that decisions regarding these resources are being irresponsibly skewed through the influence of powerful, vested interests (in commercial, political, and other categories) whose goals are not necessarily always aligned with the concerns of individuals and the people at large. . . . The Internet can be a fantastic tool to encourage the flow of ideas, information, and education, but it can also be used to track users' behaviors and invade individuals' privacy in manners that George Orwell never imagined in his 1984 world." Along with these national organizations, many state and local organizations, schools, and creative individuals continue to work to carve out innovative and non-commercial spaces on the Internet.

Communicating with Awareness

Most of the books on the topic of electronic literacy are simply how-to manuals: how to log in, surf the Web, access information, bid and shop on eBay, find love, use email, and chat with friends. Even publications that do touch on issues of a more critical sort would in the end have us believe that one is cyberliterate once one knows how to use the tools. Paul Gilster (1997), in a book with the promising title *Digital Literacy*, appears to break this mold and discuss how users can determine if a Web site is credible or not. But in the end, he suggests that digital literacy is literacy of the performance sort— that it "involves acquiring the necessary survival skills, the core competencies [described in his book] to take advantage of this environment" (28). Even when Internet software changes, you will still be "literate" if you can use the Internet to "find, verify, and incorporate [Internet] content into [your] work" (230).

Yet cyberliteracy is not simply a matter of learning how to keep up with the technology or how to do a Web search. For communication technologies shape our social and cultural spaces. Welch puts it nicely: electronic communication technologies, she argues, "have led to electronic consciousness" (1999, 104).[10] And what kind of cultural consciousness do we get from being hooked into the Internet? Consider this: oral cultures rely on storytellers, and it is necessary to be physically present to hear the story, news event, or gossip. Radio culture began with entire families listening to one program together, but in many homes today, every kid has a radio, a television, a phone, and now an Internet connection. These individualist incarnations of communication technologies inspire a completely different sense of family and community. The propensities built into computers, cell phones, Palm Pilots, and the like create new spaces in our living rooms and bedrooms.

Cyberliteracy means voicing an opinion about what these technologies should become and being an active, not a passive, participant. To become aware of technology should be to become curious. A slogan by CPSR notes: "Technology is driving the future. Who is steering?" Yet at a basic level, we are not conditioned to ask this sort of question. Note, for example, the word *user*, a standard word in technology development that describes the person on the end of the keyboard, mouse, or joystick. The term echoes throughout the software field: user-interface design, user-friendly documentation, user manuals, user error, and so on. Yet the only other area that refers to people as "users" is the area of drug addiction, where the term connotes someone who is controlled by the substance. To be cyberliterate, you need to be more than a user. You need to become an active participant in the discussion.

The cases described in this book should serve as an intellectual toolbox to encourage us to understand, critically and with awareness, emerging Internet technologies. Almost anyone can learn to create a Web site, but hardly anyone is learning to think about the social and cultural implications of emerging technologies. I address issues like flaming, emotion, and identity to encourage each of us to become better at critiquing, challenging, and anticipating how these technologies are designed, implemented, and used. We can begin these tasks by examining, in Chapter 2, some of the key features that make communication function in cyberspace.

CHAPTER 2
SPEED, REACH,
ANONYMITY,
INTERACTIVITY

Time and space, drastically compressed by the computer, have become interchangeable. Time is compressed in that once everything has been reduced to "bits" of information, it becomes simultaneously accessible. Space is compressed in that once everything has been reduced to "bits" of information, it can be conveyed from A to B with the speed of light. As a result of digitization, everything is in the here and now. Before very long, the whole world will be on disk. Salvation is but a modem away.
—Ole Bouman (1996, 1)

How does cyberspace operate? What are the "action terms," if you will, of communication on the Internet? They are speed, reach, anonymity, interactivity: the functional units by which most Internet communication takes place. These terms help us understand how cyberspace functions, how this technology is the same as and different from others before it, and how we can work with the technology to become cyberliterate.

Any given set of features cannot be applicable to all instances of Internet communication. What takes place on a Web page for teenage girls will not be the same as what takes place on an email list for professors. And what takes place in a workplace setting will not be the same as what happens when groups of undergraduates use the Internet for a class. Yet certain key features of Internet communication do seem applicable even across different circumstances. Speed, reach, anonymity, and interactivity—working often alone but mostly in combination[1]—help explain much of how we communicate online. These terms provide a framework for understanding the case examples in the chapters to follow and, more broadly, for creating cyberliteracy.

Speed and Reach

SPEED: OUR EDGY, WIRED SELVES

Two of the most obvious yet significant features of online communication are speed and reach (Figure 2.1). The combination of these two factors makes Internet communication extremely powerful. Take speed. With the split second it takes to press a single key, text, sounds, or visual information can be sent across the globe. The Internet inspires speediness. We sit poised at our keyboards, waiting for the next email message and replying as quickly as possible. People regularly apologize for not answering an email message quickly enough, and most of us have wondered if a person might be sick or out of town simply because that person did not reply right away. Speed also changes how we think about social relationships. Professors who teach online courses often mention the large amount of email they receive from students and the speed with which they feel compelled to respond. As the epigraph to this chapter suggests, speed and reach invite us to "compress time," and they do indeed create a sense that "the whole world [is] on disk" (or, today, on the Web). Whether salvation is "but a modem away" is arguable; however, the determinism that underlies this statement is obvious. Speed does not equal salvation; the speed of the Internet does not necessarily bring us closer to any sort of utopia. But speed is certainly changing how we live and what we expect, and it may be changing our mental states as well.

For example, speed is often involved in cases of techno-rage (see Chapter 3). When we expect things to be speedy and they are not, we get angry. When our Internet connection shuts down, or when a Web site takes too long to load, our emotional and physical states change. And with other technologies (cell phones, pagers, and so on) exacerbating our need for speed, we can't help noticing that speed is one of the key features of Internet communication. And this speed inspires certain behaviors and qualities.

Oralness. Part of the reason that we type messages that sound the

"First, they do an on-line search."

Figure 2.1. The power of speed and reach is characterized in this cartoon. Even these dogs know that the Internet is the place to search for information: it's fast and it reaches out widely, even beyond their sensitive sniffers. *Source:* © The *New Yorker* Collection, 1998, Arnie Levin from cartoonbank.com.

way we speak is because it's faster to type without having to worry about the formality of a written letter. Once, after being quoted in a local news story about the Internet, I received a long message on my voice mail. The caller (who didn't leave her name) was concerned about how the use of online technologies was changing students' concern for grammar and spelling. True enough: technologies that encourage an oral style will discourage attention to spelling, punctuation, and other features of print. Voice input systems, designed to speed things up even more, emphasize the trend. Our writing sounds ever more like speech, and lately, our speech has begun to sound clipped and sarcastic, like our e-writing.

Casualness. Because we can't see the person to whom we are sending a message, and because electronic texts tend to get posted with such speed, people often take a more casual approach online. When I receive email messages from undergraduates I have never met, they either don't have a salutation at all, or they begin with the very casual "Laura." Not that I mind being called by my first name, but in face-to-face settings it is unusual for undergraduates to do this. This feature has been recognized in other studies, where researchers found that students felt more open and acted more casually in an online space (Faigley 1992). Sometimes being casual turns into being angry; flaming (see Chapter 3) is related to speed, because people tend to post messages without reflecting on their content.

Redundancy. Information is often repeated online, in part because of speed. Most email users subscribe to several electronic mailing lists: work-related lists, lists related to hobbies or professional groups, and so on. It's common to receive the same email message more than once, because people often post the same message to multiple lists to be sure that their message reaches all interested parties. In addition, individual messages themselves can be redundant. On email, Usenet postings, or Web sites that allow individual comments, it has become the custom to include a previous message along with your response. This tactic is often called cascading (Figure 2.2). It's much speedier to respond this way than to recontextualize another person's thoughts in your own words.

Repetitiveness. The speed with which messages travel in cyberspace encourages messages to be sent to a wider audience than the original sender may have intended. Most people who use the Internet have had the experience of opening a message from a friend only to find that it contains a joke they first saw months or even years ago. Rumors about viruses, stories about sick children requesting cereal box tops or greeting cards, messages about health problems —these messages never seem to die. They may disappear for months but then resurface in a new round of emailing. Speed inspires us to repeat ourselves, even when we don't mean to. Speed is

```
Subject: Re: jbtc stuff
   Date: Thu, 18 Nov 1999 21:47:13 -0600
   From: "(   J___  _"·
     To: "Laura J Gurak" <gurakl@tc.umn.edu>

send the ecopy to r, and if she still needs hard copy, just send me saul's
and i'll take care of the rest.
s.
-----Original Message-----
From: Laura J. Gurak, Ph.D. <gurakl@tc.umn.edu>
To: (   J. )
Date: Wednesday, November 17, 1999 8:19 PM
Subject: Re: jbtc stuff


>Both documents look fine. The note to R. is fine also. I talked to Saul
>on the phone today, and he should have ecopy to me tonight. I told him
>I'd make the print-outs. Or, I can send you the ecopy if you'd have a
>second to make two print-outs (I will pay for them). I will send Rebecca
>an electronic copy and ask if she can accept this in the interest of
>time (Instead of a diskette. What is a diskette, anyway??)
>
>Thanks. I'll be back in touch after    '. sends me his paper.
>
>> "(   J. )         wrote:
>>
>> hello laura:
>> routing the intro and toc back to one last time--the only addition is
>> that we've added the third book review.  also, below is the text i
>> intend to send to rebecca which caps everything off.  please let me
>> know any changes before i send it and the intro and toc:
>>
>>  _____
>>
>> Dear I       :
>> Attached please find an electronic copy of our table of contents
>> (TOC.doc), our introduction (intro1.doc), and the first of our
>> manuscripts (Virtual2).  All of these files will be priority mailed to
>> you today in hard copy with accompanying diskettes and materials, as
>> directed in the Survival Kit.  If luck (or better said, the post
>> office) is on our side, a second manuscript ("striking close to home")
>> will be included as well.
>>
>> On Monday, Nov. 22, two more manuscripts will come your way ("Magic"
>> and "Interactive TV").  The fifth and final paper ("Organizations")
```

Figure 2.2. This message is both casual and redundant. Note the first section: no salutation, lowercase letters, the author's abbreviated signature ("s."). What follows is a cascade of previous messages, strung together to contextualize the note; this redundancy is something not seen in printed memos, phone conversations, or most other forms of communication. It illustrates the blur of speaking and writing that occurs in online communication. *Source:* Laura Gurak.

seductive; the repetitive posting of messages happens in part because it takes only a second to press the Enter key.

REACH: THE ULTIMATE MESSAGE IN A BOTTLE

Reach is the partner of speed. Digitized discourse travels quickly, and it also travels widely. The old telephone company slogan inviting us to "reach out and touch someone" is even more apt in cyberspace. One single keystroke can send a message to thousands of people. This message can be sent on to others, posted to a Web site, posted to Usenet newsgroups, and sent into countries with travel restrictions but no restrictions on incoming electrons. A single email message can reach more people than we realize.

Reach is also one of the "axioms of communication technology" coined by Kaufer and Carley (1993) to illustrate the power of print technology. They define reach as "the number of people within a society who potentially or actually receive the . . . communication (or set of communications)" (126). Indeed, printed documents expanded the reach of information far beyond that of traditional oral communication. A book could be circulated far more broadly than an oral story. Reach is even more important in discussing the Internet, because electronic discourse can reach thousands, even millions, and it can do so quickly. And reach, like speed, inspires certain behaviors and qualities.

Multiplicity. As Kaufer and Carley (1993) note, multiplicity is the number of people with whom you can communicate at one time. "Mass communication technologies," they correctly observe, "all have high multiplicity" (103). The broader the reach, the more people will see the message. Nowhere is this more evident than on the Internet. In the controversies over Lotus MarketPlace and the Clipper chip (Gurak 1997), one single message reached thousands of people in a day. Today we see the same phenomenon when we receive the same joke message several times in one day from several people. Multiplicity drives ecommerce, because the base of people to whom one can sell things is suddenly made up of everyone with an Internet connection. One Web site, whether of a giant company or of a small home business, can reach millions.

Globalness. Marshall McLuhan's "global village" is apt here, because the reach of online technologies does indeed give us a sense that the world is a far smaller place. Bouman's words quoted in the epigraph should be updated to read "the world [not salvation] is but a keystroke [not the soon-to-be outdated modem] away." Globalness is related to multiplicity; both concepts involve electronic information reaching many people. But globalness is also related to issues of culture and to who is doing the sending. Most Web sites originate in the United States, and the issue of globalness poses a critical question for cyberliteracy: How can we make this new literacy become something more diverse than U.S. ideas and values being spread throughout the world?

Lack of gatekeeping. Try as one might, it is almost impossible to restrict an electronic idea. The reach of online communication means that traditional gatekeepers—news editors, government censors, parents—probably cannot control information much longer. During the war in Yugoslavia in 1999, for example, the Internet was a far richer site of information than any news station. One reporter described the situation as "the first instance of warfare where a small but significant slice of the population has Internet access," noting that many Yugoslav citizens "used the Web to create an entire news network consisting of email exchanges, chat rooms, and bulletin boards—where no rumor is too small to dissect at length and almost no hamlet too remote to mention" (MacFarquhar 1999).

Countries that place tight restrictions on information, like China, have difficulty dealing with the power of reach. If just one email posting or Web site from a country under siege makes it onto the Internet, it will reach far and wide in just minutes or, at most, hours. And while this feature could change depending on shifts in who controls the Internet, still, the very structure of the Internet encourages a non-hierarchical communication form. The early Internet was designed so that if one hub in the network went down, others would be available. Messages could be routed to their destinations via many different paths. Thus, once a message hits the wires, it is hard to control.

Visual reach. The concept of reach includes more than just the number of people who see a message. Reach often involves multimedia: visual, oral, and written discourse. Most Web pages use color, sound, images, video, text, and icons to express their message. And this mixed palette means that people with various levels of reading ability, visual acuity, and comprehension can be reached.

Logotypes or icons have often been used to reach those who do not read (Figure 2.3). As Welch (1999) notes, "Icons were a hallmark of nonliteracy. Public houses in England, for example, were marked by representations of objects, such as the Lion and the Rose, as well as by the writing of those words. Those who could not read could understand the icon" (117). In addition, icons are useful

Figure 2.3. Icons and symbols have long been used to communicate to audiences with varying levels of reading ability and different native tongues. This German icon, dating from 1907, was used to indicate a print shop. *Source:* F. H. Ehmcke, *Graphic Trade Symbols by German Designers from the 1907 Klingspor Catalog* (New York: Dover Publications, 1974).

for crossing language barriers; international symbols are the only way to navigate in an airport where you don't speak the language, and even on the computer, icons (mostly Microsoft's) are becoming a universal language.[2]

Community. Reach enables us to form communities of common interest across vast distances. Interactive Web sites are now available on almost every topic imaginable: hobbies, current events, health problems, research interests, rock bands, television shows, and so on. Many Internet observers have written about the notion of on-line community, and for a while, a debate ensued as to whether these spaces and interactions really counted as community. In my study of Lotus MarketPlace and the Clipper chip (Gurak 1997), I argued that the sites and interactions associated with these pro-tests did indeed constitute a new kind of community. As with physi-cal communities, network participants were located in the same "place." Instead of being situated in a physical forum, however, this community was located in an electronic and virtual place where people with common values gathered around an issue and took ac-tion. As in all communities, participants were linked by these com-mon values, yet in the virtual world, these links were not limited by physical distance or time. Participants moved easily from place to place, forming and reforming communities with a fluid and dy-namic quality.

Others have argued that these virtual spaces are not community but "lifestyle enclaves," false versions of community that "provide only the sense of community" (Doheny-Farina 1996, 50). But ongo-ing examples continue to suggest that old, physically bound notions may need to be expanded in order for us to recognize the ways com-munity plays itself out in virtual space. In 1999, when a young woman in rural Minnesota was kidnapped from a convenience store (the evidence was plain to see on the store's videotape), a Web site (www.findkatie.com) quickly sprang up in response. This site was firmly rooted in the physical community of her hometown, but it was also a community for the world. People from across the globe posted thoughts to a guest book, and the site helped recruit search volunteers from all over the state and beyond. The power of reach was evident, and the connection to the physical was obvious. This was a positive example of online community, one that strengthened local ties and reached out globally as well.[3]

As in the physical world, the dark side of community is present online as well. Communities attract people of common interest. Thus, hate groups also use the Internet for their communities. These sites reinforce dangerous, violent values in a way that existed before the Web but is made easier by the reach of cyberspace (see Chapter 3).

Anonymity and Interactivity

Speed and reach are features of many electronic technologies. The telegraph is still speedy; radio, television, and the telephone are quick, too. Any time that ideas travel electronically, they will necessarily be delivered with greater speed than surface delivery can achieve. Of course, speed and reach—for all the reasons listed— are more extreme in cyberspace. But two other features, anonymity and interactivity, make the case for cyberliteracy even more clearly.

ANONYMITY: "IS THIS THE PARTY
TO WHOM I AM SPEAKING?"

A now-famous *New Yorker* cartoon shows two dogs working on a computer, and the caption reads, "On the Internet, no one knows you're a dog." This cartoon reminds us that sometimes you really never know who is at the other end of an electronic text. It could be a man posing as a woman, a child posing as an adult, a robot posing as a person, or even a dog posing as a human. The power of the computer to mask identity, gender, and other features has been discussed since the early days of computing. In the 1960s, for example, Joseph Weizenbaum of MIT was both impressed and cautious about how people responded to the automated therapist program known as ELIZA. Janet Murray, in *Hamlet on the Holodeck* (1997), recounts how the vice president of a company thought, when communicating with ELIZA, that he was interacting with a real person (69–71). Today we can never be sure about whether the "party to whom we are speaking" is Lily Tomlin's telephone operator, our best friend, or an automated response system. Anonymity in online space inspires us to consider several features.

Identity. This has always been a key feature in human communication. People who study communication and rhetoric remind us that we make judgments about the credibility of an argument based on the credibility of the speaker, and for thousands of years, this rhetorical appeal—known as ethos—was based on knowing who the speaker was. In oral cultures, listeners can see the speaker. With printed texts, readers can imagine the author (even if he or she uses a pseudonym). On television and the radio, audiences see a face or hear a voice and come to feel that they know the speaker. But in cyberspace, the identity behind what you see floating on the screen is not always what you imagine.[4]

You may ask yourself how this is different from a book's author using a pseudonym. Despite a growing understanding about online communication, people still seem to have a greater expectation that on the Internet, they are communicating with a real person of that name. The community and intimacy that the Internet inspires can create an erroneous trust in any new virtual friends we may have made. In addition, the ability to interact with people online heightens our sense of who they are. And in electronic space, it is easy for a single person to assume any number of identities—something far more difficult for an author to do.

No one has brought this issue to our attention like psychologist and computer critic Sherry Turkle. Her book *Life on the Screen* documents the nature of identity on the Internet, particularly among students who spend a great deal of time in real-time role-playing games (called MOOS and MUDS). She notes that identity becomes fractured, multiplied, and magnified in cyberspace. She describes what happens as people play these games, communing with others and changing personalities through the use of new screen names: "They become authors not only of the text but of themselves, constructing new selves through social interaction. One player says, 'You are the character and you are not the character, both at the same time.' Another says, 'You are who you pretend to be'" (1995, 12). The issue of changing identity has broad implications for cyberliteracy.

The most famous case of the power and problems associated with anonymity and identity switching is what the researcher who studied it called "the strange case of the electronic lover." In this case, a man in an online discussion list disguised himself as "Joan," a psychologist who had been in a car accident and was confined to a wheelchair in her apartment. Her only contact with people was through the computer. After others on the list got to know Joan, offering support and sharing intimate secrets, she was revealed to be an ablebodied man who had assumed this identity in order to see "what it felt like to be female." List participants were extremely angry at this deception (Van Gelder 1990, 128–129). Today we must learn to recognize that it's naïve to assume that anyone in cyberspace has any particular characteristic. To be cyberliterate is to be cautious when considering identity.

Digital identity is tied in with ecommerce. It is not as easy to be anonymous on today's Internet as it was in the early Internet days. A sequel to the *New Yorker* dog cartoon appeared in a Detroit newspaper in spring 2000 (Figure 2.4). This cartoon was a reminder that even when you think no one knows who you are, background software, especially on ecommerce sites, is gathering information about you. So although you can skew your identity in cyberspace, others may be collecting information about you at the same time.

Gender and sex. In most cultures throughout the ages, humans

Figure 2.4. An update to the famous *New Yorker* Internet dog cartoon, illustrating the actual complexities of anonymity on the Internet. *Source:* Toles © *The Buffalo News.* Reprinted with permission of Universal Press Syndicate. All rights reserved.

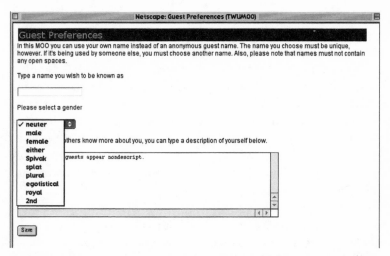

Figure 2.5. Like most MOOs, the Texas Women's University MOO (TWUMOO) provides users with a choice of genders far greater than mother nature ever considered. Source: moo.twu.edu.

have made initial judgments about a person based on that person's sex. We look at the other person, make a decision, and proceed to communicate with that person as a man or as a woman. For a time, sex was considered a fixed trait, determined by genitalia, hormones, and genes, while gender was considered more mutable, based on social characteristics. And we now know that sex is also more complicated than the simple male-female distinction—a fact that people who hang out in the real-time simulated spaces called MOOs (which stands for Multiple user dimension, Object Oriented) have known and experienced for years. Most MOOs give participants a range of gender choices when first connecting; on the Texas Women's University MOO, for example, participants can be neuter, male, female, either, Spivak, splat, plural, egotistical, royal, or 2nd (Figure 2.5). Surely these options imply great changes in literacy: our words and thoughts, our speeches and artwork, are often linked to us as gendered beings. And this most basic of concepts is quite different in cyberspace from the way it is in the physical world.

Authorship and ownership. The identity-based concepts of *author* and *owner* are problematized in the digital world. It is often difficult to identify the authors of a digital document. Email contains the cascading parts of other messages. Web sites contain material gleaned from other sites as well as links to images, other Web pages, sounds, and text. From one perspective, this makes for a wonderful space where information can be shared, reused, and circulated. But when authorship and ownership are as fluid as this, notions about what constitutes plagiarism become confusing. Students read the standard "do not plagiarize or else" statements in a course syllabus, but they are surrounded by a technology that encourages them to use others' material freely. Issues of copyright also become critical. In an information-driven economy, it is all well and good to have a technology that promotes sharing, but those who stand to gain by keeping their materials to themselves and out of the public domain do not like the idea of free information (see Chapter 6).

Just because it is possible to be anonymous in an online chat or with a new email account does not mean that such anonymity is guaranteed. In several cases, courts have ordered Internet providers to reveal the true identities of online individuals. When employees of Raytheon Corporation posted business information on a Yahoo Web site, for example, company executives became concerned. In 1999 a court ordered Yahoo to reveal the true identities of the individuals who had posted the information.

Ownership also has political implications. In the early days of the Internet, when domain names (such as gurak.com) were free for the asking, anyone could assume any identity. As companies began to notice the business potential of the Internet, and as the custom of not using cyberspace for commercial purposes disappeared, companies began registering their domain names. Some were shocked to discover that their corporate names were already taken. For example, a site belonging to 12-year-old Chris Van Allen, www.pokey.org (Figure 2.6), was a surprise to Prema Toy Company, which makes the flexible children's toy called Pokey. (In this case, courts decided that Van Allen could keep the domain name; hundreds of Internet users from around the world logged in to Chris's site to register their support.)[5] Yet soon thereafter, "anticybersquatting" laws be-

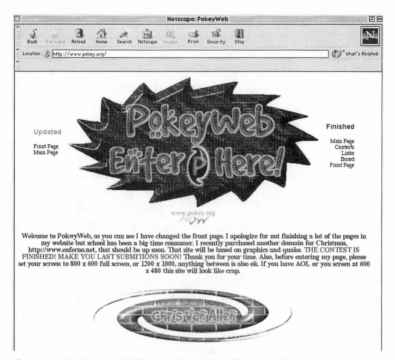

Figure 2.6. Twelve-year-old Chris Van Allen's "Pokey" Web site. *Source:* www.pokey. org.

gan to be introduced and passed, making it a crime for someone to knowingly register a domain that contains the trademark name (such as Pokey, McDonald's, or Sony) of another person or company. Most courts have sided with those who already hold the trademark or copyright (usually a large commercial interest). In some cases this seems fair, but in the case of sites that existed first or sites related to a person's name or hobby, this trend is unbalanced and counter to the free and open spirit that makes the Internet so exciting.

Flaming. When no one can see you, and your identity is masked, it is easy to be ruder than you might be in a face-to-face environment. And because it is so easy to switch identities, you can be rude as one identity, then suddenly disappear and become someone else.

One of the most significant features of cyberliteracy is interactivity. Unlike television, online communication technologies allow you to talk back. You can talk back to the big company or you can talk back to individual citizens. You can reach inside the box of images and sounds and become part of the glowing neon colors. You can share opinions and recipes, join a discussion, get a direct connection to a project, or send your good wishes to others. One of the biggest potentials of cyberspace is the potential to be a two-way street in a world where the dominant medium (television) has been unidirectional. In turn, interactivity inspires us to consider several features.

Access to the inner circle. What sort of literacy is implied and enacted when readers and writers, creators and audiences, have so much opportunity for direct contact and communication? Throughout history, people have often wanted to meet the writer of their favorite book or at least to have some connection to others who read the work. Book groups are limited by time and space, but online sites are not. And in a cyberliterate world, everyone is an author. My Web site is a rhetorical artifact, and anyone who sees it can send me email and engage in a discussion. Stepping through the printed page was never possible, but stepping through the screen is an everyday occurrence. The interactive nature of online technologies lets us be on the inside of the discussion.

The capacity to talk back. Direct communication is not only about pleasant discussion. Interactivity, and the lack of gatekeeping on so many sites and spaces across the Internet, means that we can talk back to anyone and everyone with an email address. This ability to interact, combined with the encouragement we feel because of the speed and reach of the medium, encourages talking back: to companies, professors, students, CEOs, other citizens, experts on a variety of topics, and regular people we have something in common with but have never met. Some of this talk can be friendly and civil; other messages can be angry and rude. Regardless of tone, interactivity invites a sense of the public that we may have forgotten: although people may not have the time or energy to attend local town meetings, they do seem to like to speak out via the Internet. Thus "talking back" also inspires community: in talking back, citizens can form communities of common interest.

A two-way presence online. What if all Web pages were simply computerized versions of books, articles, or magazine pages—text and graphics, maybe some sound, and links to other documents on the site—with no interactivity? As on many Web sites today, individuals would probably still establish their online presence by way of sites about their new baby, family news, individual ideas, or collections of their poetry. In fact, in pre-Web days (the days of Lynx and an Internet that was purely text-based) individuals did create their own discussion groups. But there was no way of knowing who saw the site, and plain text was not very appealing. Part of any communication is having an audience, and it is the lure of an audience of millions, and an audience that can write back to you, that drives many people to create Web pages. This two-way presence happens because of the interactive nature of cyberspace technologies.

Ecommerce and connections to the customer. When it comes to talking back and interacting, many companies are realizing the power of the Internet. Amazon.com, an ecommerce site with one of the largest customer bases, is a good example. Its site offers multiple ways for customers to interact, including customer service email addresses, Web-based forms, and plenty of discussion spaces for readers' thoughts and ideas. Customers can talk to Amazon.com employees, and they can commune with other customers. But, as one observer noted, some organizations are still cautious about allowing open communication: on many sites, it is impossible to find a phone number with which customers can contact the company (Bermant 1999). In the summer of 1999, for example, I signed up for a local digital subscriber line (DSL) service. After learning about hidden costs and other annoying features (the loss of my second phone line for voice, for example), I tried finding a customer support number on the company's Web site. No luck. In fact, this site did not even offer an email address for customer information. In this case, the company had decided that it did not want to take advantage of interactivity; instead, its Web site was like a printed page or a television commercial. This troubling choice gave me even more reason to cancel my order. (Eventually, I did find an email address buried within a company press release.)

Privacy. The more interactive a site, the greater the potential for privacy problems. A site that allows you to enter personal information in return for a purchase may use this information in ways you can't imagine. Every day, new ideas and regulation schemes are proposed to deal with issues of privacy, but in the end, Internet technology allows so many different ways to collect and use information that no one will be able to find a simple solution.

In the remaining chapters, I rely on the key terms of speed, reach, anonymity, and interactivity to examine key trends in cyberspace and to help articulate the issues critical for cyberliteracy.

CHAPTER 3
TECHNO-RAGE:
MACHINES, ANGER,
AND CENSORSHIP

You post a note to a Usenet newsgroup or a Web chat room. Suddenly, you
find your email box flooded with rude replies from people you've never met.
They call you names, insult your intelligence, and chastise you for posting
such stupid questions: "flaming you," in Internet terms. Or: you connect to a
Web site looking for information about a recent political event, but all you
find is highly opinionated pages full of sarcasm and anger. Welcome to the
world of techno-rage: a place where our machines make us mad.
—Laura Gurak, keynote address (October 1999)

In this introductory comment from a keynote presentation, I
attempted to give my audience a sense of what I meant by techno-
rage. But I barely needed to make the case. Everyone was nodding
his or her head in agreement. They all knew what it meant to be
flamed, because at one time or another, each person had experienced this feature of life in cyberspace. When I went on to discuss
flaming in the context of other events, like road rage and annoying
voice message systems, the audience seemed to agree that our machines, marvelous as they can be, seem to contribute to an ethos of
edginess, anger, and sarcasm.

Unlike paper, electrical devices pulsate at you, humming their
electrical songs and inviting you to go along for a ride at high
speeds. Speed, one of the action terms of cyberspace, is seductive:
the more you have, the more you want (see Chapter 2). The highly
charged pace of an email exchange, for example, seems to encourage us to send more and more messages, far beyond what we could
or would do on paper. Often, such messages are sent without much
thought on the part of the sender; sometimes, anger that might be

cushioned by the slowness of a paper document rebounds around cyberspace before the sender has a chance to reconsider. The quickness with which we can connect to the Web and download information also inspires us to want more: more information, more speed, more connections. And when the speediness stops, lessens, or is interrupted, we may become angry—often angry enough to hit the computer screen or keyboard.

Marshall McLuhan, employing his idea of "light through," observed that television screens put us into a hypnotic trance; media critic Paul Levinson, McLuhan's former student, argues that computer screens also invoke this sort of hypnosis (Levinson 1999). Yet computer hypnosis, unlike that with television, is not passive. It is interactive, speedy, and seductive. The pulsating screen, which provides beautiful images and sounds, also may act like a giant vacuum sucking away our physical energy and increasing our tension and anger. Can we do anything about this? First, we must recognize the symptoms and trends of angry, edgy speed.

Everyone in the wired world has experienced the edgy side of speed: Web sites that don't load, voice telephone trees that make you wait, cell phones and pagers that beep in the middle of a lecture or a movie, modems that rarely connect at the speed promised on the box. Often I find myself sitting with fingers poised over the keyboard, waiting while a Web page loads and feeling my blood pressure rise with each passing second. The anger felt while waiting for a voice mail system to pick up or email to download is insidious, because the technology is maddening but nonetheless invites us to continue. It is the speed we love to hate, and it has clear implications for cyberliteracy.

One study describes the fatigue factor associated with computer use. According to this study, while the number of computers in homes is rising, actual computer usage may be dropping. The reason given: "technology-weary users prefer to wind down and spend time with their families rather than interact with office-like PCs" (Arbitron Pathfinder Study 1999; see also Chapter 8). Similarly, being online may make some people prone to depression. A study by researchers at Carnegie Mellon University suggests that the more time people spend online, the more depressed or socially with-drawn they become (Kraut et al. 1998). Some would even say that too much time spent in the physically disconnected, speedy spaces of the Internet is contributing to the overall lack of civility and decorum.

It is hard to say which factor is the cause and which the effect. But our technologies do have consequences, and being cyberliterate involves recognizing connections between the technologies of the Internet and who we are. This certainly includes the relationship between Internet use and our emotional states.

Road Rage Everywhere

The current zeitgeist of edgy, angry behavior was characterized by one commentator as "the Y2K social disease . . . the anxiety that is going to be produced when telecommunications combines with the 'Evernet'—the technology that will soon allow people to get online from their watches, their cars, their toasters, or their Walkmans—so that everyone will be connected all the time, any time" (Friedman 1999). This state of constant connectedness leads us to become wired and edgy in everyday life. Constant ringing and buzzing may produce more efficiency, but they also keep us in a pumped-up state, like the jittery caffeine high that at first may be fun but then becomes irritating. Everywhere—at home, at school, and at work—we are surrounded by speedy, blinking, beeping technologies. In my large lecture classes, I need to remind students to shut off their pagers and cell phones. In offices, as one news story reports, meetings never end, because co-workers continue to send each other instant messages (Slatalla 1999). Many studies confirm that the number of email messages we receive, particularly in the United States, is on the rise, and as our machines converge so that not just computers but also cell phones, Palm Pilots, and other devices will allow us to download email and connect to the Web, we can easily see a time when it will become hard to escape the digital noise.

This hyped-up state of affairs can and does lead to physical manifestations of anger, as any news story on road rage will show. Perhaps one of the most appalling of these events occurred in Minneapolis during the summer of 1999, when a medical doctor driving a BMW became stuck behind an older woman who, he thought, was taking too long to get on the highway. He pulled over, approached her car, and punched her in the face through the open window. He then proceeded to leave on a trip to Europe; upon his return, he was arrested. Part of his retribution involved attending anger management classes.

The computer seems to be part of this trend. In one survey, computer users reported shattering the monitor, breaking the mouse, or kicking the hard drive while waiting for the computer to respond (Concord Communications 1999). We have tasted high speed, and we like it. And we grow impatient with our machines when things do not go quickly enough. We also grow impatient with other people, and on the Internet, we express this anger through a style known as flaming.

Flaming: Road Rage on the Information Highway

Most of us have been flamed by an angry co-worker, a student with bad manners, or a perfect stranger who belongs to a discussion list. Flaming is the online manifestation of road rage: people get angry and use harsh language to get even.

A standard definition of flaming comes from computer-mediated communication researcher Martin Lea and colleagues (1992), who define it as "the hostile expression of strong emotions and feelings" (89). They argue that flaming is "overreported" and perhaps not as common as the popular press would have us believe. Yet in terms of cyberliteracy, what matters is not quantity: one flame can affect the ethos of an entire discussion list or Web site. Flaming may not be as common as we assume, but it does happen, particularly in certain contexts (as Lea and colleagues also argue) and under certain conditions.

The following exchange is a classic flame. In this posting to a list for technical writers, a popular site where writers exchange information and ask questions related to their work, someone asked the following question:

PLEASE TELL ME THAT USING TASK AS A VERB IS NOT BECOMING POPULAR!

DOES ANYONE ELSE SAY THIS? WHAT'S THE STORY HERE?

This simple question evoked the following reply:

I HAVE A BRILLIANT IDEA FOR YOU. LOOK IT UP IN THE DICTIONARY BEFORE YOU SEND A MESSAGE OUT LIKE THIS! WHILE *YOU* MAY NOT LIKE IT, THE USAGE OF TASK AS A VERB WAS PERFECTLY VALID. DO SOMETHING MORE WORTHWHILE WITH YOUR LIFE THAN CRITIQUING E-MAIL MESSAGES. STOP ASSAULTING MEMBERS OF THE LIST WITH YOUR WORTHLESS RHETORIC AND YOUR STUPID PET PEEVES!!

This reply fits the definition of a flame according to the Electronic Frontier Foundation (EFF): "A particularly nasty, personal attack on somebody for something he or she has written." Several features in this example are classic markers of a flame:

- The use of sarcasm ("brilliant idea").
- The personal tone ("you," "do something more worthwhile").
- The generally rude tone ("Look it up in the dictionary").
- The use of oral features, such as capital letters (shouting), extra exclamation points (increased vocal pitch, emphasis), and asterisks (again for emphasis).

Ong's (1988) observation that oral discourse is agonistically toned is evident here, and perhaps the hybrid written-oral nature of some online communication, combined with the speediness of wired texts, creates the perfect situation for flaming. Other action terms of cyberspace are also evident in this message and in flaming generally: reach means that anyone who wants to let off some steam can do so to a huge audience; interactivity means that you can talk back if you are angry; anonymity means that you can disguise yourself and send hateful messages that you will never have to defend.

Other standard reasons for flaming, described by other researchers and categorized by Lea and colleagues (1992, 92–94), include the following:

Lack of social cues. When people cannot see each other, they lack the social cues of body language, communication norms, and so on that govern many communication situations.

Computer culture. Some argue that the caffeine-driven world of computer hackers was the basis for early instances of flaming. This style grew out of the youthful (some would say immature), irreverent culture of UNIX programmers.

Gender. Most of these early programmers were male, and several researchers have argued that flaming is a male style of communicating (Herring 1993). (Gender and flaming are discussed in more detail in Chapter 4.)

Whatever the reasons, flaming has always been a part of cyberculture and is often viewed as a sort of art or sport. There is even a newsgroup dedicated to flaming (alt.flame). And some rules of "netiquette" even say that flaming is an accepted, acceptable part of being on the Internet:

> Rule 7: Help keep flame wars under control
> "Flaming" is what people do when they express a strongly held opinion without holding back any emotion. It's the kind of message that makes people respond, "Oh come on, tell us how you really feel." Tact is not its objective.
> Does Netiquette forbid flaming? Not at all. Flaming is a long-standing network tradition (and Netiquette never messes with tradition). Flames can be lots of fun, both to write and to read. And the recipients of flames sometimes deserve the heat.
> But Netiquette does forbid the perpetuation of flame wars—series of angry letters, most of them from two or three people directed toward each other, that can dominate the tone and destroy the camaraderie of a discussion group. It's unfair to the other members of the group. And while flame wars can initially be amusing, they get boring very quickly to people who aren't involved in them. They're an unfair monopolization of bandwidth. (Shea 1999)

Is this point of view acceptable? Perhaps not in terms of a cyberliteracy that values inclusivity and civil discourse. Take the following case: In May 1999, more than 25,000 faculty members and students at Stanford University received an email message containing racial slurs directed at African American and Hispanic students. This message and others like it go beyond the kind of verbal jousting of most flames and become hate-filled weapons designed to intimidate and cause more anger. The speed and reach of cybertechnology allowed the message to land quickly in thousands of email boxes. And, in a telling use of anonymity, the sender of the Stanford message had pirated a student email address, making the message appear to come from a particular student when it did not (Mendels 1999). Hatred is bad enough, but when this sort of hatred is spread widely and when the author hides behind an anonymous email address, we have crossed a line from verbal jousting to overt racism and extreme anger.

To be cyberliterate requires us to ask about the communication norms of online space. Flaming may sometimes be no more than a short verbal joust between two people with too much time on their hands, but some research indicates that flaming is mostly male and that this style excludes women. Flaming may also exclude people who are new to the Internet (often flamed for being "newbies"), because these people unwittingly violate the norms of acceptable speech in online space. And in some cases, full-blown flames may incite even more anger. For example, the continuing rise of extremist sites suggests that flames can be fanned into full-blown fires.

Extremist Sites: Flaming Web Pages

For the past several years, as computers have become cheaper and anyone can suddenly become a desktop publisher, we have witnessed a rise of extremist Web sites in the United States. In these cases, we see an extreme version of flaming and, in addition, the dark side of online community. Community, one aspect of reach, can be a powerful way for people with similar interests to come together and share ideas (see Chapter 2). Many observers have noticed the power of online community not only to reach out to the world but also to create cohesion and solidarity among a regional community. (In Chapter 2, I describe one such site: findkatie.com, set up to help coordinate efforts and spread the word concerning a young woman from northern Minnesota who had been kidnapped.) Yet the ability to link with like-minded people and form community can have a dangerous side. Because of the power of speed and reach, and because of the value we place on free speech (a right of U.S. citizens and one that pervades the ethos of cyberspace), extremist Web sites exist side by side with all the millions of other Web displays, all equally available with just a few keystrokes.

To some extent, these sites reflect an anger and disempowerment that have become noticeable in the United States at this time. Domestic terrorism is at an all-time high, and angry people, primarily white males, are banding together like never before. These groups can hide behind a Web site, with its wide reach, relying on the power of anonymity to keep them from the people they don't wish to face. Yet in terms of cyberliteracy, these sites are frightening because their messages are hateful, angry, and violent in tone.

How can we judge these sites in an attempt to think about cyberliteracy? The first and most obvious way is to consider them in legalistic terms.

Unprotected Speech: The Case of the Nuremberg Files

The prevailing legal standard is based on the liberal enlightenment model (the foundation for philosophy and laws of free speech in the United States) and holds that all ideas should be given equal voice in the press and other information media. In this model, it is expected that citizens will in the end weed out good ideas from the bad. This model has generally functioned well, in part because it is hard to think of alternatives: censorship rarely works for any length of time, and in an electronic age censorship is even more difficult to enforce (see Chapter 6). Ever since the Tiananmen Square uprising, when information flowed outward via fax and the Internet (despite government attempts to control it), it has become evident that information is global, not local—or, as some hackers like to say, "information wants to be free."

But despite this emphasis on free speech in the United States and on the Internet, some speech is simply not legally protected. The standard by which the courts make this decision is based on the idea that certain words can be dangerous and harmful to people. It uses the standard of "shouting fire in a crowded theater": Would the speech bring about violence against others? Language that incites violence is often ruled as unprotected. It is upon this standard that we currently make legal decisions about hate speech and the Internet.

One example that illustrates how the legal standard can be used to judge an extremist site is the case of the Nuremberg Files, a Web site created by an anti-abortion group. This site used "Wanted"-style posters to list the names, addresses, and license plate numbers of physicians who performed abortions. The Web page was designed with a special interactive feature: when a physician on the list was killed, his or her name was struck through with a red line. On 2 February 1999 a federal district court ruled that this site was not protected speech. The jury determined that the site was intended to incite violence and murder; one piece of telling evidence was the listing of Dr. Barnett Slepian, a physician from Buffalo, New York, who was murdered and whose name had a line drawn through it on the Web site.

Web sites and other online discourse (email messages, Usenet postings) can thus be judged according to their legality. By legal standards the Nuremberg Files Web site was not acceptable. It was not protected speech because it incited physical violence and death; with the wide reach of Web pages, this standard is important to uphold. Online stalking can also be judged by legal standards. When one woman spurned a male co-worker's sexual advances, he posted notes on the Internet that looked as though they were being posted by her. These notes included the woman's address, phone number, and information about her home security system. They also suggested that she had fantasies about being raped. Through the power of reach, these notes spread over the Internet. Legally, this action was judged unacceptable: in January 1999 a judge in Los Angeles convicted the man under a new anti-stalking state law.

Anti-Information: The Case of AmeriCorps and the Objectivists

Many other sites may represent legal, protected speech but would be considered disturbing to the average person. Anti-Semitic, racist, or homophobic sites that encourage paranoia, anger, and hate can fall into this category. Most of us can spot the obvious ones, such as sites asserting that the Holocaust never happened, or sites that encourage overt bigotry or racism. But some sites are less obvious, and this layer of sites must be carefully examined if we are to consider the meaning of cyberliteracy. Many of these sites masquerade as informational, adopting the format and style of a newspaper, report, or other truly informational setting. They use professional-looking fonts, high-quality layouts, and other credibility-boosting devices that are easy to employ on the Web. But to be cyberliterate means to be able to look past the format. Just because a site looks good or seems neutral and informational does not mean it is so. The powerful visual tools (fonts, layout, graphics) of the Web make everything look "real," and the ability to link to other sites enhances this sense of credibility. As one commentary noted, "racist pages are growing in sophistication and may lure the unwary" (Marriot 1999).

Therefore, a different, cyberliterate way to view Web sites is not only via a legal standard but also via a moral one. Although most forms of speech are protected, not all forms of speech are morally or ethically acceptable. An event from my electronic life makes this argument.

One morning, innocently enough, a discussion began on our department email list that soon became a perfect case for analyzing the trend of calling clearly biased sites "informational." That morning, our College Career Services director posted a note announcing that representatives from AmeriCorps, the volunteer program for college students, would be visiting campus.

As mentioned earlier, what is especially disturbing about many extremist sites is that they pretend to be informational. Yet by now, most people who teach or theorize about writing know that there is no such thing as purely informational writing. Instead, we know that all language has a voice and an opinion, and that all language wields power. So when a student suggested that a site linked to the philosophies of Ayn Rand was a valid counterpoint to the posting about AmeriCorps (see Figure 3.1), I was moved to get into the debate.

When I viewed the suggested site, I was immediately disturbed. It was apparent that this site was not simply a "source of information"

Re: AmeriCorps Information Session
Date: Thu, 11 Nov 1999 11:15:34-0600
From: _____ <anyone@ourdept.umn.edu>
To: _____ <student@tc.umn.edu>, <classlist@rhet.agri.umn.edu>

I found the following site to be a good source of information in opposition to
the AmeriCorps program:

www.aynrand.org/no_servitude/

> The following announcement is compliments of _____ of Career
> Services.

> Come learn about the experience of a lifetime!

> AmeriCorps Information Session
> Thursday, November 11, 4:00 PM
> 345 Fraser Hall
> OSLO Conference Room

> AmeriCorps is a national service program that provides opportunities
> for people of all ages to make a difference in their communities.
> AmeriCorps members serve in low-income communities working
> to address critical needs in the areas of education, environment,
> economic development, technology, health, housing, public
> safety, etc. During their full-time service, individuals receive a
> living stipend, have health coverage, and earn an educational award
> of $4,725 to pay for loans, college, or further education.

> College students can join AmeriCorps after graduation, or gain
> experience during college by taking a year off to serve.

> Come learn about full-time service opportunities available with the
> AmeriCorps*VISTA (Volunteers in Service to America) and
> AmeriCorps*NCCC (National Civilian Community Corps) programs.
> Applications are now being accepted. Fall and Spring Graduating
> Seniors, or students interested in taking a year off to serve, are
> encouraged to apply.

> AmeriCorps Walk-in Office Hours
> Mondays & Thursdays 1:00–3:00 PM
> Wednesdays 9:30–10:30 AM
> 310 Fraser Hall

Figure 3.1. The original email posting about AmeriCorps. It seemed innocent enough
but inspired a discussion about hate sites when one student suggested that an extremist site was a valid counterpoint. *Source:* University of Minnesota, Rhetoric Department discussion list.

to use for comparison with the posting about AmeriCorps. It was an extremist view, unbalanced and revealing an underlying ethos of anger and hate. I felt compelled to post a note indicating that such an extremist site was not a good counterpoint, and in my note, I also injected a bit of opinion about Ayn Rand's objectivist movement. After all, an academic list is a site of free speech, and as an Internet critic with a cyberliteracy agenda, I feel it's important to make strong claims to counter the prevailing winds of commercialism and individualism pervading the Internet. Like many departments, we often have such exchanges on our mailing list. My email set off a flurry of messages, mostly in response to my classifying the site as a "hate site." Some students saw the obvious connections, but others were not convinced, swayed as they were by the look and feel of the site: nice graphics, a supposedly bona fide organization, links to other sources, and so on. Yet a quick analysis shows that this site (Figure 3.2) shares many features with the more overt extremist sites. In some ways, examining this site is more useful than looking at the more overt ones, because such an examination illustrates the subtlety needed for cyberliteracy.

This site, purportedly sponsored by advocates of objectivism, is more subtle than sites often classified as extremist, because at first glance it does not seem to employ overtly hateful tactics. But as with many extremist sites, this one uses an informational mode to disguise its message as credible; notice, for example, that it employs traditionally informative genres, such as press releases and position papers. Also, the page has a nice design and an appealing layout. Yet a quick analysis identifies this site as one inspired primarily by anger, not facts. The largest and most prominent image on the page is a photo of a group of protesters holding signs featuring such extreme language as "slavery" and "Nazi." Many extremist sites associate themselves with Nazism in some way, and even though this site is using the term to describe AmeriCorps, the word itself is evocative of hatefulness.

Moreover, the association of AmeriCorps with "forced servitude" illustrates a hyperbolic, paranoid, angry ethos, one that is often evident on extremist sites. The very premise that the AmeriCorps program equals "forced servitude" is flawed, because AmeriCorps is a

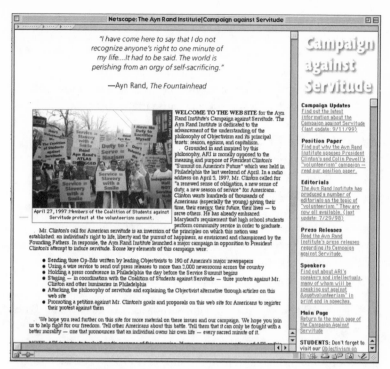

Figure 3.2. This site, filled with hyperbole, anger, and trigger language (like "Nazi"), is not a purely "informational" site. But it's hard to realize this without some analysis, because the site hides behind nice graphic design and lots of external links. *Source:* www.aynrand.org/no_servitude.

volunteer program: no one is forced to join. Real servitude, as in slavery, is quite a different thing from joining AmeriCorps, the Peace Corps, or any other volunteer organization.

Like most extremist sites, this one exhibits the following characteristics:

Anger. Most extremist sites are set up to vent anger. Unfortunately, the people who create these pages often fail to realize that anger inspires action. Words like *Nazi, slavery,* and *servitude* do not inspire open discussion; instead, they make those who believe those words even more angry, and they make those who don't hold this point of view upset as well.

Paranoia. It is common on these sites to read about government conspiracies; for example, this site refers to President Clinton's views as "call[s] for American servitude."

Mob or group action. Most extremist sites inspire mob action. In this case, the crowd of students in the photo feels more like a mob than a peaceful protest because of the angry messages on their signs and the exaggerated use of "Nazi" and "slavery."

Hyperbolic claims. Extremist sites usually make exaggerated claims. Suggesting that AmeriCorps is "forced servitude," for example, is baseless, because no one is forced to volunteer for the organization.

Self-referentiality (citing and linking to similar groups). Extremist sites often provide links that look like outside information but actually connect to other like-minded thinkers. In this case, the links on the right side of the page are links to other materials from the Ayn Rand Institute.

In terms of cyberliteracy, a legal standard is of no use here, because this site does not directly suggest violence or harm to others. Shutting down this site because we do not agree with it is a bad idea and would certainly be a step on the slippery slope of censorship. Instead, the standard for cyberliteracy should be a critical one. To be cyberliterate in our system of free speech, we must learn to read, view, and think critically. We need to be aware that Web sites that are set up to sound "informational" always have a point of view, and that sometimes this point of view can be cause for concern, especially if it goes unexamined. Furthermore, although the Web constitutes a vast source of information, it is self-referential in a way that no other communication medium can be, because it can continually update its links. This self-referencing can be a problem: linking to similar ideas encourages a closed debate, one that does not admit conflicting viewpoints.

Filtering Out the Anger

The Anti-Defamation League (ADL), among other groups, has reported on what it calls "the dark side of the Internet"; in particular, the ADL is concerned about how hate sites can be used to recruit new followers, particularly young people. Many people who teach speech and writing have begun to notice that more and more students want to give a speech or write a paper about some "informational" topic, which turns out to be based on "information" from one of these hate sites ("proving," for example, that the Holocaust did not occur).

One approach to the problem is the use of filters, such as the ADL's HateFilter (Figure 3.3). Although filters can help, they have limits. Filters that search for the word *Nazi* can filter out accurate, scholarly information along with the extremist sites. Perhaps for young children, such filters are one tool parents can turn to. But for adults, a more useful filter begins with cyberliteracy, because cyberliteracy requires us to take more than just a legal stance when it comes to evaluating online spaces. It requires us to speak up when we encounter sites masquerading as informational and to teach our children, friends, students, and colleagues about the consequences of online anger. Furthermore, it requires us to counter these spaces by developing and supporting sites that embody inclusiveness, civility, and scholarly ideals.

Another approach is suggested by legal scholar and Internet theorist Lawrence Lessig. Lessig agrees that judging Web sites by legal standards alone is not enough. He makes this claim for a slightly different reason: because the Internet is global, laws about protected speech in one country are not the same as laws in another. Speech that promotes the Nazi party, for example, is illegal in Germany but not in the United States (1999, 166). Lessig argues that at the level of "code"—that is, by tinkering with browser software—individual users can customize their profile to filter out information they don't wish to see, and that this approach is preferable to broad governmental efforts to regulate speech. In the United States, one such effort was the Communications Decency Act of 1996, which Lessig (1999, 174–185) calls "a law of extraordinary stupidity" and which was later overturned by the Supreme Court. This law would have regulated speech—particularly pornography—on the Internet. But the court rejected this approach, viewing it as too broad, vague, and dangerous to the first amendment.

The Information Superhighway Needs A Crossing Guard.

INTRODUCING

at www.adl.org

Your child can learn anti-Semitism, racism and terrorism right in the comfort of your own home. On the Internet, the KKK is calling for an America of, by and for whites only. Neo-Nazi skinheads are advocating a "holy war" against their enemies. Holocaust deniers are claiming "no execution gas chambers existed in any camp."

That's why we've created Anti-Defamation League HateFilter. It's a software product parents can install on home computers to prevent children from gaining access to World Wide Web sites that advocate hatred, bigotry and violence.

ADL HateFilter is unique because it doesn't just block sites, it offers kids the opportunity to link directly to the ADL site to get information about the nature of hate and the people and organizations who promote it.

Check **www.adl.org** for more information on how to get ADL HateFilter. Because you don't want bigots teaching your children.

Anti-Defamation League, 823 United Nations Plaza, New York, NY 10017   **www.adl.org**

Figure 3.3. The Anti-Defamation League encourages the use of filters as a way to screen out the hatred and bigotry of some Web sites. *Source:* Anti-Defamation League (ad run in several national newspapers), www.adl.org. Reprinted with permission of the Anti-Defamation League.

Lessig is correct in arguing that laws should not and cannot be used to regulate speech online. Yet what his approach ignores is the very point made by my example of the AmeriCorps debate. Filters and personal profiles could, if refined from their current states (filters, in particular, still are not perfect), do a fine job of removing sites that you don't want to see before they ever reach your computer. But they enhance the ability of people to stay within their own communities, reading only the things that already support their frame of reference. The angry students who support the objectivist site could easily filter out any information that they find contrary and view only those sites that support their stance. The same thing would be true for everyone—people with liberal, communitarian, or left-wing viewpoints would read only what they like, people who are anti-abortion would encounter only those ideas that supported their frame of reference, and so on. And people who are already hostile would grow even angrier if all they encountered were hate and extremist sites. Filters, then, may have their place, but they do not support a full cyberliteracy, one that believes in open information but asks Internet citizens to turn a critical eye on whatever information they encounter.

Anger and Cyberliteracy

In the end, cyberliteracy means rejecting technological determinism. Even though the key features of online communication—speed, reach, anonymity, interactivity—may inspire or encourage us to behave in certain ways, in the end we, not the machines, are in charge. The edgy, wired times we live in do not necessarily have to translate into all-out anger. Cyberliteracy means understanding the tendencies of Internet communication and making thoughtful, informed choices. You can stop yourself from flaming someone just as you can stop yourself from saying something hateful in person. Many companies, organizations, and electronic lists or Web spaces have created rules of netiquette for their individual sites rather than succumbed to the draw of the technology. Even the netiquette rules cited earlier (the ones that said flaming can be all right), suggest some humanity in Rule 10: "Be forgiving of other people's mistakes."

Even if you do use filters, you should be aware of a range of discussions and points of view, and you should voice your opinion when you do not agree. Another approach might be to engage extremist sites in class exercises or as a topic of discussion at work or with your family. Because cyberspace has such a global reach, enhances communities over vast distances, and encourages discourse among lots of people, we need to learn more tolerance, not less. Cyberliteracy means being open but critical. Speak up. Create ways to assess online anger. Get away from the machine for a few minutes each day. Find ways to live in a world of ideas but not a world of hatred.

In addition, it is important to support legislation that helps increase the tolerance and goodwill of cyberspace. For example, the California law that makes online stalking a crime should be considered at a federal level, because currently only one-third of all states have such laws. And while laws can help, cyberliteracy also means being aware that computer technologies and the Internet are not neutral. We build our biases into technology, and we bring our social conditions into online space. The next chapter illustrates how this takes place in terms of gender.

From my earliest effort to construct an online persona, it occurred to me that being a virtual man might be more comfortable than being a virtual woman.
—Sherry Turkle (1995, 210)

There is no race. There is no gender. There are only minds on the Internet.
—MCI television commercial (1997)

Why did Sherry Turkle, after extensive research and experience with online life, feel that being a virtual man might be easier? Although MCI and others would have us believe the Internet is a utopian space where gender does not count, this is not the case. It is questionable both how much access women have to computers and how women and girls are treated once they get online. The answer, some would say, is right there on the Internet: if you don't like being female, just change your screen name to a male one. Yet although gender swapping may be easy, this does not negate the misogyny, gender bias, violence against women, and stereotypes that exist online. Cyberliteracy requires a critical eye toward gender and the Internet, with thoughts on how to make it a more inclusive space.

This chapter explores how gender is embedded, switched, invented, and challenged in the online world. We begin with a gendered history of the Internet, which is based in military technology and was invented in the male military culture of the 1960s.

Cyberspace as Gendered Space

Technologies are not neutral in value. They carry the marks of their makers and the ethos of the culture in which they arise. The

Internet is no exception. Our current iteration of the network and the discourse it inspires are not neutral in any sense. On the contrary, the features of our social spaces are often heightened online. For example, our commercial, capitalist model for new technologies is clear: instead of being developed as a place for democratic discourse, education, and community, the Internet is quickly turning into an enormous home shopping network. Gender biases, just as in real life, are evident online. Yet for many years now, we have lived with the mythos of the Internet as a neutral space where anyone is free to say anything. The MCI television commercials from the mid-1990s, quoted in the epigraph to this chapter, touted the magical ability of the Internet to banish all social ills. "There is no race," someone claims, as a montage of faces flash by. "There is no gender," says yet another bright-eyed Internet believer. All that exists in this wonderful world of bandwidth and bytes is, they tell us, "the mind." Only the mind full of value-neutral ideas, ready to engage in high-spirited conversation, information exchange, and true communication. Probably the most characteristic representation of this Cartesian, gender-neutral simulacrum is a now-famous *New Yorker* cartoon ("On the Internet, no one knows you're a dog"). Yet as the update to this cartoon illustrates (see Figure 2.4), there are many ways to tell who's who on the Internet these days (more on this in Chapter 6).

This vision of the Internet as a cure for our social ills is popular, especially for companies trying to sell online access to the yet-un-connected, and it has shaped our notion of what to expect from this new technology. Yet this vision is in stark contrast to what often happens on the Internet. The rhetoric of these commercials does not always match the real situations that exist for women and girls online. From many standpoints, cyberspace can be seen as distinctly gender biased. It is easiest to support this claim by first reaching back and painting the landscape in which the Internet was developed.

A Gendered, Rhetorical History of the Internet

Few of us know the history of the Internet and the landscape in which this technology developed. We don't always consider that any technology starts in a particular place and time. An analysis of this history helps us see the gendered roots of the Internet. As many people now know, the Internet was originally developed by scientists and engineers in the late 1950s as a Department of Defense technology. Given that the technology arose in the domains of science, engineering, and defense during the 1950s, it is no surprise that the Internet was created by men. Even today, science and engineering fields are dominated by men, and many scholars have examined this issue (Hornig 1989; Noble 1992; Turkle and Papert 1990). Because technologies are created by people and within the norms of a given period, a history of the Internet must ask about the culture of this time, particularly the culture of the engineering world.

There are many ways to approach this question, but one, a rhetorical analysis, involves stepping back and examining several representative artifacts from that time and culture. A series of articles from an engineering newspaper serves this purpose quite nicely. These columns, titled "From the Boss's Lap," are from two 1954 issues of the newspaper *The Rensselaer Polytechnic*. This newspaper was (and still is) the campus paper of Rensselaer Polytechnic Institute, in upstate New York, one of the oldest and most prestigious engineering schools in the world. After World War II, GIs flocked to Rensselaer and other institutions to become engineers and take advantage of the scientific, technology-driven, postwar economic boom.

I analyze these two pieces not to pick on Rensselaer, which was my graduate institution and of which I am very fond. Rensselaer in the 1950s is just one snippet of the broader cultural landscape of the time. It represents the state of engineering culture in the postwar period, which is precisely the period during which the Internet was being conceived and designed. As such, these two pieces provide a snapshot of women, men, and the Internet at a formative time.

The column "From the Boss's Lap" was presumably a vehicle for the author, one George G———, to highlight certain of the women on campus.[1] In both examples, these women are not engineering students but rather clerical help. The first article (Figure 4.1) begins:

From The
Boss's Lap
By GEORGE G

"Rensselaer Poly-technic Library, Mrs. M J S speaking," answers a low sultry voice. Behind this voice is a tall, fair complexioned country lass. You've all seen M J walking 'round the library, with a twinkle in her eye and an obliging smile playing on her face.

It's an unusual chain of events that would bring a girl from a small farming town in the mid-West to a library in RPI. You'd know that it would take an RPI man to swing this deal. M J was born in W. - Iowa, on 9, 1932.

M J says that wasn't much of a social center, and there wasn't much to keep a cute girl busy. M J later went to Iowa State where she majored in Home Economics. Ever get that feeling that you just want to be some place else? M J did, and found herself work for the United Airlines Company in San Francisco. From there it was a short step to RPI At a Servicemen's center, M met a Marine, and on Ap-ril 1952, M J married R S

Like many GI's, R felt that going to school at Uncle Sam's expense was a good deal. He applied to RPI, and entered as a Freshman as an Electrical Engineer in February, '53, for it had then been a policy at RPI to allow Frosh to enter in February. M J applied for a job at school, and received a position at the library.

M J is secretary to Mr. C , head of the library. She types, takes telephone calls, and does other usual duties. M J adds that Mr. C is one of the nicest hosses she's ever had. She is a great cook, likes to play the piano, and has traveled over most of these United States; 35 to be exact.

" " as she's called at home, is 5' 4", weighs 110, and has an interesting 34-23-34 figure.

Transit . . .

(Continued from Page 1, Column 5)

9:45 Acacia

Wednesday, December 8
8:15 Managers Club
8:30 Alpha Epsilon Pi
8:45 Zeta Psi
9:00 White Key Society
9:15 RPI Players
9:30 International Club
9:45 Sigma Chi
10:00 Sigma Phi Epsilon

Figure 4.1. A column from an engineering student newspaper in the 1950s. *Source:* "From the Boss's Lap," *Rensselaer Polytechnic* 75 (24 November 1954): 5.

"Rensselaer Polytechnic Library, Mrs. M——— J——— S———
speaking," answers a low sultry voice. Behind this voice is a tall,
fair complexioned country lass. You've all seen M——— J———
walking 'round the library, with a twinkle in her eye and an obliging smile playing on her face.

It's an unusual chain of events that would bring a girl from a
small farming town in the mid-West to a library in RPI. You'd
know that it would take an RPI man to swing this deal.

The article goes on to describe M——— J———'s background in
home economics and her experience meeting her husband, an
electrical engineering student at RPI. The article concludes with:

"Stevie," as she's called at home, is 5′ 4″, weighs 110, and has an
interesting 34-23-34 figure."

This column is not an exception; it ran each week. Another issue
of the "Boss's Lap" asks:

Why is everyone so anxious to fill in forms, ask questions, and just
loiter around the Army ROTC office in Winslow? The answer is
the pert Miss C——— B——— C———, as she's called by students and faculty alike, one of the hottest numbers on the RPI
campus! With her black hair, little pug nose, and a swooney figure, no wonder guys have traded in their ten minute coffee break
for this campus cutie.

We then learn that C——— is

nineteen years old, tips the scales at 110 pounds, and stands 5′ 5″
with nothing on. Her vital statistics are 34, 24, 33. If we haven't
convinced you yet, C——— lives at 112 F——— Court, Troy.
She's as close as your telephone at AS2-7166.

Needless to say, the column would never be seen today, and these
excerpts, in particular the listing of an address and phone number,
would probably be classified as sexual harassment, invasions of privacy, and more. Yet in those times, it was standard to think about
women this way, and in an all-male engineering environment, the
sexism and objectification in these pieces would be particularly un-
noticeable.

It was within this landscape that the Internet developed. In 1968 the developers of the first DARPANET wrote an article describing their vision for this technology. In some ways the article is forward thinking in its ability to suggest how we might use the network for community building, research, and so on; one cartoon in the article shows two people flirting via email in a manner suggestive of many Internet advertisements today, thirty years later. But at the same time, the article offers a clear picture of the gender bias of the authors and the times. The title of the magazine itself is suggestive: *Science and Technology: For the Technical **Men** in Management* (emphasis added). The article (Licklider, Taylor, and Herbert 1968) uses a cartoon to illustrate how computer users employ mental models (Figure 4.2).

There are many ways to illustrate this notion of mental modeling, but the choice of a woman in a bikini (which is later removed, presumably leaving her naked) is clearly a biased one. This cartoon woman could easily be one of the many fine lasses featured in "The Boss's Lap"; like those articles, this cartoon puts the emphasis on the woman's figure, not her personality or her mind.

This background against which the Internet was developed can-

"When mental models are dissimilar, the achievement of communication might be signaled by changes in the structure of one of the models—or both of them"

Figure 4.2. This cartoon accompanied an article about the Internet written by the men who developed the technology. *Source:* Licklider, Taylor, and Herbert 1968.

not be ignored. The postwar landscape of engineers focusing on bits, bytes, and women in bikinis was where it all began. No small wonder that early UNIX commands included words like *abort* to stop a computer process. And no wonder women are still having difficulties gaining access to cyberspace.

Women and Access to Online Space

Some observers might argue that things are not so bad today; after all, that was the 1950s, and now women are using the Internet in greater and greater numbers. A 1998 study by the Pew Research Center for the People and the Press supports this line of thinking, indicating that "women are joining the ranks of Internet users, who not long ago were largely well-educated, affluent men."

Yet a quantitative measure is only one way of considering the issues of access. Even if more and more women are using the Internet, this trend does not ensure equal access or a lack of gender bias.

Janet Gardner (1999) has argued that there are many level of access. First is the material level: Do women have access to the needed hardware and software? This is the most popular way to think about access. But there are several other levels to consider:

Temporal. Do women have time to learn the technology and the conventions for interacting online?

Linguistic. Does the Internet require any special language that may be unfamiliar to the novice user?

Topical. Do perceptions of the Internet mirror reality; in other words, do the gender biases in real life spill over into cyberspace? And are alternate points of view welcome?

Psychological. Does the Internet allow women to feel comfortable, and can women identify with the goals, values, and styles on the Internet?

It is these last two items, topical and psychological, that give rise to further consideration of gender in cyberspace. For while it may be true that more and more women are using the Internet, issues of topical and psychological access may still make it a place that is non-inclusive—a place in need of cyberliteracy.

Flaming as Gendered Behavior

Even as women gain material access to cyberspace, significant barriers to true equity remain. The history of Internet development is decidedly male. It is reflected in the general engineering culture of the time (the pert Miss C——— B———) and in the specific culture of those who created the technology (woman in bikini). In some ways, gender bias is built into the fibers and cables, into the protocols and switches, and into the subsequent computer culture and language habits that arose in these spaces. Thus, it is no surprise that as Internet use became more widespread (from the late 1980s to the mid 1990s), certain gendered interactions began to occur.

Linguist Susan Herring (1993), who is well known for her studies of gender online, has made the case that flaming (see Chapter 3) is in some part a gendered style of communicating. In one study of an academic mailing list, or listserv, she noted that men participated more than women, and that when women did contribute, their language was attenuated and meek, while men's language was assertive and imperative. Men made more statements, whereas women asked more questions. Men were more sarcastic and self-promoting, while women often asked supportive questions and made apologies for themselves and their thoughts. Although Herring and others note that it is impossible to generalize from individual studies, it is clear that flaming is often a male style of communication.

It is easy to spot this pattern throughout cyberspace. Another analysis of the example of flaming from the technical writer's list presented in Chapter 3 illustrates this point. In Chapter 3 I left out the issue of gender, but I will add it here to make the case. (As noted in the Appendix, I have changed the names of the original writers.)

The original posting was written by Sandy:

PLEASE TELL ME THAT USING TASK AS A VERB IS NOT BECOMING POPULAR!
DOES ANYONE ELSE SAY THIS? WHAT'S THE STORY HERE?

The first reply was written by George:

I HAVE A BRILLIANT IDEA FOR YOU. LOOK IT UP IN THE DICTIONARY BEFORE YOU SEND A MESSAGE OUT LIKE THIS! WHILE *YOU* MAY NOT

LIKE IT, THE USAGE OF TASK AS A VERB WAS PERFECTLY VALID. DO
SOMETHING MORE WORTHWHILE WITH YOUR LIFE THAN CRITIQUING E-MAIL
MESSAGES. STOP ASSAULTING MEMBERS OF THE LIST WITH YOUR
WORTHLESS RHETORIC AND YOUR STUPID PET PEEVES!!

The next posting was written by Barb:

SANDY,
   DON'T LET ONE PERSON'S TIRADE GET TO YOU. I SAW NOTHING
WRONG WITH YOUR QUESTION ABOUT "TASK" AS A VERB. I THINK HE
MAY HAVE THOUGHT YOU WERE NIT-PICKING SOMEONE'S EMAIL MESSAGE,
RATHER THAN ASKING A GENERAL INTEREST QUESTION.
   I HAVE FOUND OUT MYSELF, THE HARD WAY, THAT IT IS VERY EASY
TO BE MISINTERPRETED ON THE NET. THAT'S WHAT MAKES EMOTICONS
SO IMPORTANT. :-)
   BARB

Here we see all the markers of gendered communication. Sandy
posts a message asking a question, and George replies with a classic
flame, echoing many of Herring's observations (assertive, sarcastic,
and rude to boot). Then Barb posts a supportive note to Sandy,
opening with a salutation, supporting Sandy's original request, and
ending with a smiley face. This use of such emoticons as smileys is often a feature of women's discourse, used to deflect the tension of a
situation and provide a bit of comfort for the reader. In my study of
Lotus MarketPlace (Gurak 1997), I found that most people using
emoticons were women.

Why is it the case that in so many instances, men are doing the
flaming? Part of the answer lies with the history of the Internet. The
"Boss's Lap" attitudes of engineering culture made their way into
early computer culture, and when the Internet was being developed, these attitudes mixed with a developing tone of independent,
often surly UNIX programmers. It was these programmers and their
successors (those who learned the system, such as computer science
students, researchers, technical experts, and scientists) who were
the early Internet users. Even as the Internet began to reach a wider
audience (especially after browsers were invented and America
Online took off), the attitudes and rhetorical styles set in place by

the early users became the operating standard for all cyberspace. Things may be changing today, as a more and more diverse population comes online, but the language of cyberspace, like any language, retains much of its linguistic roots.

Another reason why flaming may be a male style of communicating is that cyberspace is not the utopia described by all the media hype. Instead, life on the Internet is like real life. Such books as *You Just Don't Understand* (Tannen 1991) and *Men Are from Mars, Women Are from Venus* (Gray 1992), in addition to volumes of other published research, note that men and women have different styles of communicating. These styles are part of the Internet, because the Internet, in the end, is made up of people and our habits. And these styles are even more evident online because of the strong male bias built into the Internet from the start.

Sadly, even when women do move away from making attenuated assertions, they are still subjected to misogynist attitudes. This is often true even if the woman in question has a highly technical background, as in the case of Dorothy Denning (Gurak 1997). Professor Denning, then head of the computer science department at Georgetown University, dared to take a stand in the debate over the Clipper encryption standard. She did not agree with the majority in the protest, who felt that the Clipper standard was an example of Big Brother in action. Denning, who was one of several experts asked by the federal government to analyze the proposed Clipper standard, favored the government's proposal. Responses to her opinions were characterized by misogyny; at one point she was referred to as "the Wicked Witch of the East." Thus, she was flamed (or, perhaps, burned at the virtual stake) for asserting her opinion, and flamed with a phrase reserved for powerful women who are feared by a hostile culture.

Are steps being taken to include women in cyberspace? Are women being persuaded to use the Internet, and is there any chance for an inclusive cyberliteracy in this regard?

Barbie, Hot Wheels, and the Death of Purple Moon

From an early age, both boys and girls are being invited to the computer through their daily experiences. Before kids can walk or talk, they witness their parents pushing buttons and making things work, watch the microwave reheat a meal, or listen as the cell phone rings. Many of today's infants spend time near the computer as parents, siblings, and friends surf the Internet. These children will be more fully digitized than any generation before them. And yet their invitations to the computer are loaded with gender bias. Perhaps most overt are two computers made just for kids: the pink and flower-power "Barbie Computer Designed Just for Girls" and the blue box painted with a bright yellow flame (!) called "The Hot Wheels Computer Designed Just for Boys" (Figure 4.3). Each comes with a bonus item: for a girl, it is a digital camera (keeping her behind the lens, a passive observer), and for boys, a steering wheel and foot pedals (keeping him in the driver's seat, in control on the information highway). It is no coincidence that these outrageous stereotype reinforcers are brought to us by none other than Mattel, makers of Barbie software and the corporate force partially behind the demise of Purple Moon software.

Purple Moon began with great promise. The company was started in 1996 at Interval Research Company (www.interval.com), a Silicon Valley think tank owned by Paul Allen, co-founder of Microsoft. The creative force behind Purple Moon was Brenda Laurel, a computer interface designer and researcher who was already well known for such books as *Computers as Theater*. Laurel spent several years studying how girls interact and play with computers. What she determined was that girls found the "play, die, and start over" model of so many boy-oriented computer games to be boring. Instead, girls preferred narrative, collaborative games, games that were not overly "pink" like Barbie but that did not emphasize violence, either.

Purple Moon software was designed based on Laurel's findings. Two games, "Rockett's New School" and "Secret Paths in the Forest," were released in September 1997. The games starred Rockett (Figure 4.4), an eighth-grader whose interactions with the other game characters involved narrative structure, emotional and social issues, and the development of personal character. The games were praised in the media and by parents and children alike.

All along, Purple Moon's arch-rival was Barbie; Barbie software

Figure 4.3. Barbie computers are pink, and Hot Wheels are blue. (The headline has since been modified to read "Computers for Kids.") *Source:* Advertisement run in many national newspapers and on the Internet during late fall and winter 1999.

Figure 4.4. Rockett, the fated character of the Purple Moon line of software. *Source:* Purple Moon Software, www.purple-moon.com.

was the major player in girl games, and Purple Moon was a far smaller company. Purple Moon faced what one writer called "an unforgiving battle for shelf space with Mattel," which owned most computer games designed for girls and which dominated the retail market (Harmon 1999). In 1998 Mattel's "Barbie Photo Designer" sold $12.9 million worth of products, while Purple Moon grossed a mere $1.6 million. In the end Purple Moon could not compete; despite its fine product and appeal to a new standard for girls and computing, in March 1999 the company was acquired by Mattel. Purple Moon software is still available (www.purple-moon.com), but Barbie is the key player. The pink Barbie computer comes loaded with many software packages, but Rockett and her friends are not among them.

This is not the first time Barbie has been a problem for women and technology. In 1992 the new "Teen Talk Barbie" sparked a small but powerful Internet uprising when women and men took to cyberspace to protest one of the doll's sayings: "Math class is tough." After several months of widespread Internet discussion, Mattel relented and changed the doll's programmed saying. But that was a small win; today's Barbie computer only exaggerates the problem and ensures that it will persist.

The Purple Moon approach is not perfect. In fact, marketing only to girls may reinforce stereotypes and behaviors that keep girls out of engineering and computing in the first place. As one journalist for *Wired* magazine put it, "Pushing girls into their own corner of the stores—and selling them make-up, shopping, interactive diaries, and reformatted girls' books—also moves towards the territory of old-school gender dichotomy" (Brown 1996).[2] In fact, another movement—grrls—asserts an entirely different ethos. These Web sites and games, such as "Tech Girl's Internet Adventures"

"It all started when I typed hello."

"Amber" got into Prodigy Chat on Thursday, 11:38 P.M. · TIME TO GET ONLINE · A PRODIGY · TIME TO GET PRODIGY ·

Prodigy Software for **WINDOWS**™

Figure 4.5. Amber, an invitation for men to join the fun of the Internet.
Source: Prodigy Software, www.prodigy.com.

(www.girltech.com), present wired, energetic, assertive female characters who don't seem the least interested in lipstick or diaries. This approach may represent an improvement on either the pink Barbie model or the what-girls-want Purple Moon model. Yet in the end, the Barbies still outweigh the cybergrrls in quantity, money, and power.

What other images of women reside in cyberspace? Besides Barbie and Rockett, another theme is represented by "Amber," from a free Prodigy disk from 1996 (Figure 4.5). "Amber," who looks like a porn image, is clearly inviting not women but men to join her. And she certainly does not make women feel invited for their brains. Instead, she reminds us of the "Boss's Lap" column. Amid amazing technological inventions and possibilities, women are still viewed primarily as sex objects. In this world of the Internet, women's bodies count more than their brains and expertise. Pornographic images still abound online; in many cases, if you make a typo while entering a Web address, you end up at a pornography Web page.

Identity and Gender Swapping in Cyberspace

Some would say that the answer to the gender disparity on the Internet is to do away with concepts of gender altogether, and that cyberspace holds the key to this plan. Digital technologies do provide opportunities for humans to interact while disguising their gender. On many real-time chat sites, such as MOOs (real-time chat spaces described in Chapter 2), male participants can log in as female, females can easily assume the character of a male, and both men and women can participate as an "it" or other neuter gender (see Figure 2.5). The ability to change identity in cyberspace presents a new way to consider gender. Maybe if we can remove gender references altogether, women will have more access to online spaces.

It is true that switching gender via the Internet can be an enlightening experience, and many online participants have reported new insights when they logged in as the opposite sex. But these experiences are by no means utopian. Why, for example, did Turkle (1995, quoted in the epigraph to this chapter) feel that it would be easier to be a man than a woman in cyberspace? Several cases illustrate why, and these cases remind us that technology alone will not eliminate the social complexities associated with gender bias and computing.

In one case, a man tricked a group of women into thinking that he was "Joan," a lonely house-bound woman with no friends other than her virtual ones (see Chapter 2). In the world described in the MCI commercials and touted by other Internet pundits, virtual gender swapping such as this is harmless and offers a perfect way to explore what it might be like to be the opposite sex. But the Internet itself is no guarantee of gender equity or anonymity. In the Joan case, some of the giveaways about Joan's true identity were her aggressive attitude and her focus on sex. Lindsay Van Gelder (1990), the author of the widely cited essay on this case, describes the revealing factors this way:

> The truth is that there was always another side to Joan's need to be needed. She could be obnoxiously grabby of one's time. [After she kept making demands on my time], I had to get blunt— and I felt guilty about it, since Joan, after all, was a disabled woman whose aggressive personality was probably the best thing she had going for her. (My first sexist thought, when I found out that Joan was really a man, was "Of course! Who else would be so pushy?") . . .
>
> Joan was sexually aggressive. Every woman I interviewed reported—and was troubled by—Joan's pressuring to have "compusex." This is online sex, similar to phone sex, in which people type out their hottest fantasies while they masturbate. . . . Her m.o. . . . was to establish an intense nonsexual intimacy, and then to come on to them, usually with the argument that compusex was a natural extension of their friendship. (135–136)

Thus, even in a space where women and men can swap identities and explore gender, this exploration is not value-neutral. Men, even when disguised as women, still exhibit classic male traits; in this case, aggressiveness toward women and their time, and attempts to turn a friendship into an excuse for a sexual experience. This case is only the tip of the iceberg. Most women who sign onto a real-time chat or MOO with a female name can report more than one time when they received private messages from males, asking them for a date or inquiring into their social status. But if those women log in with a male identity, the harassment quickly stops. Cyberspace is not cut off from the everyday sexism of the regular world. Or, as Van Gelder says, "maybe one of the things to be learned from . . . Joan is that we have a way to go before gender stops being a major, volatile human organizing principle—even in a medium dedicated to the primacy of the spirit" (1990, 142). Perhaps another lesson is that we like to *think* that the Internet is "dedicated to the primacy of the spirit," but in fact it tends to reflect and even heighten many of our real-life social concerns.

Cyberliteracy and Genders

Cyberspace, then, is certainly not a utopia when it comes to gender. The history of the Internet sets the stage for the current state of affairs, and given the Barbie computer of 1999, it is hard to argue that things are getting any better. So what can we do? Barbara Warnick (1999), while noting the sexism of computer culture, observes that women are increasingly more comfortable with the Web and are in fact building their own sites, "constructing welcoming places where invitational discourse becomes truly inviting" and where such images as "Amber" are replaced with "cybergrrls" (16). Cyberliteracy requires us to acknowledge the gendered nature of the Internet and to take action. We can construct sites that defy this trend, reject Barbie computers, create new role models for girls and women, and recognize that there is no utopia, even in cyberspace. The next chapter, illustrating the problems of hoaxes and myths, continues to articulate these central lessons for cyberliteracy.

CHAPTER 5
HUMOR, HOAXES, AND
LEGENDS IN CYBERSPACE

LITTLE JESSICA MYDEK IS SEVEN YEARS OLD AND IS SUFFERING FROM AN ACUTE AND
VERY RARE CASE OF CEREBRAL CARCINOMA. THIS CONDITION CAUSES SEVERE
MALIGNANT BRAIN TUMORS AND IS A TERMINAL ILLNESS. THE DOCTORS HAVE GIVEN
HER SIX MONTHS TO LIVE. AS PART OF HER DYING WISH, SHE WANTED TO START A CHAIN
LETTER TO INFORM PEOPLE OF THIS CONDITION AND TO SEND PEOPLE THE MESSAGE TO
LIVE LIFE TO THE FULLEST AND ENJOY EVERY MOMENT, A CHANCE THAT SHE WILL NEVER
HAVE. FURTHERMORE, THE AMERICAN CANCER SOCIETY AND SEVERAL CORPORATE
SPONSORS HAVE AGREED TO DONATE THREE CENTS TOWARD CONTINUING CANCER
RESEARCH FOR EVERY NEW PERSON THAT GETS FORWARDED THIS MESSAGE. PLEASE GIVE
JESSICA AND ALL CANCER VICTIMS A CHANCE. IF THERE ARE ANY QUESTIONS, SEND
THEM TO THE AMERICAN CANCER SOCIETY AT ACS@AOL.COM.
—Email chain letter listed on U.S. Department of Energy page
  (ciac.llnl.gov/ciac/ciacChainLetters.html#jessica)

From cellular phones that might make gas pumps explode to
virus email messages that will crash your computer to sick children
in need of greeting cards, rumors and hoaxes abound on the Internet. Anyone with an email account quickly notices that certain messages seem to make the rounds. Hoaxes asking you to send a card to
a dying child or to save box tops from cereal so that a family won't
starve are popular. So are messages about deadly computer viruses
that will wipe out your hard disk. These messages come disguised in
language that make them seem credible, but they are almost always
false. In addition, humorous messages—workplace humor, political jokes, not-so-funny puns—from your brother, your distant
cousin, or a friend you have not seen in years may also appear in

your email box, prefaced by a long list of others who've also been forwarded this message. You're expected to join in the fun and forward the note along. Yet these messages waste bandwidth and clog people's email boxes unnecessarily.

What makes people circulate humor and hoaxes? Is there something about the technology that encourages us to keep passing these along? And how can people distinguish between what is credible and what is not? A cyberliterate citizen is one who knows how to be critical about online information. As the Internet continues to grow, it will be important to distinguish facts from hype, especially because much of the hype is designed to create fear and alarm. Speed, reach, and anonymity combine in cyberspace to inspire the spread of all sorts of information. This chapter examines the whats and the whys of online myths: what they are and why they spread.

Categories of Online Hype

It is helpful to distinguish among the various types of much-forwarded messages, because each type exhibits different qualities. By knowing one type from another, you can spot these messages more easily.

One Web site suggests the following categories of messages:

- Hoax = False, deliberately deceptive information, including pranks
- UL = Urban Legend: a popularly believed narrative, most likely false
- Rumor = Questionable or erroneous information forwarded with gusto
- Junk = Flotsam and jetsam of the Net (Emery 2000)

The Computer Incident Advisory Center (CIAC), a reputable source on this subject, narrows down this list, suggesting three categories: hoaxes, chain letters, and viruses. In addition, several other pesky forms of online communication are worth noting. A broad review of the subject reveals the following categories: hoaxes, chain letters, jokes and humor, viruses, and inaccurate Web pages.

Some etymologists suggest that the word *hoax* is derived from the word *hocus* (as in "hocus-pocus"). The connotation of "now you see it, now you don't" is useful when thinking of Internet hoaxes. These messages may look credible, but usually they are nothing more than smoke and mirrors. The compelling language, designed to draw you in and make you feel that the message is real, usually cannot be backed up with real facts.

You can separate hype from the truth by using some simple rhetorical analysis. The CIAC suggests that two features in particular make for a successful hoax: technical-sounding language and what they call "credibility by association." Probably one of the oldest hoaxes around is the "Good Times Virus." This message (Figure 5.1), which a group of students is said to have originated in 1994, resurfaces every so often.

This message contains both technical-sounding language ("erase your hard drive") and credibility by association (an indication that

Happy Chanukah everyone, and be careful out there. There is a virus on America Online being sent by E-Mail. If you get anything called "Good Times", DON'T read it or download it. It is a virus that will erase your hard drive. Forward this to all your friends. It may help them a lot.

The FCC released a warning last Wednesday concerning a matter of major importance to any regular user of the InterNet. Apparently, a new computer virus has been engineered by a user of America Online that is unparalleled in its destructive capability. Other, more well-known viruses such as Stoned, Airwolf, and Michaelangelo pale in comparison to the prospects of this newest creation by a warped mentality.

What makes this virus so terrifying, said the FCC, is the fact that no program needs to be exchanged for a new computer to be infected.

Figure 5.1. The widely circulated "Good Times" Virus.
Source: www.doctormac.net/Viruses/Goodtimes.html.

the Federal Communications Commission released a warning about the hoax). What most people, especially those new to the Internet, fail to realize is that it is not possible to infect your computer with a virus simply by reading an email message. Email attachments can contain viruses, but viruses have yet to be transmitted via a plain-text message.

In addition, some hoaxes use a personal style, making it seem that the message was generated by a real person with a real affiliation to a real company or organization. One example is the "AOL V4.0 Cookie" hoax (Figure 5.2). Not a bit of this message is true. Yet it circulated widely, in large part because of its personal style. Note how it opens: "I'll try and cut through the crap, and try to get to the point of this letter." This sentence conveys the strong personality of someone who is perhaps a bit angry and who definitely has something to say. The message continues with this personal tone, appealing (like many hoaxes) to a disease or personal plight of the author ("Unemployed, with one of us going through a divorce [me] and another who is about to undergo treatment for Cancer"). Also, the continued use of the grammatically incorrect "me" instead of "I" ("me and 2 of my colleagues"; "as me and my colleagues discovered") gives this note a sense of having been written by a real person. Another item that makes this hoax a success is, as with the previous example, its use of technical-sounding terms ("examining and debugging the program"; "deep in the program code").

Another set of clues about hoax email comes from the Stiller Research News site:

- All capital letters with many exclamation points in the title. This is typical of most of the hoaxes (and many scams!) that we see.
- A warning to avoid email with a particular title. Almost all of the virus hoaxes contain this type of directive.

CHAIN LETTERS

Chain letters can also be hoaxes. In other words, a hoax may often be written with the plea that readers pass on the message to everyone they can think of. According to the CIAC, "chain letters all

From a former AOL employee:

I'll try and cut through the crap, and try to get to the point of this letter.

I used to work for America Online, and would like to remain anonymous for that reason. I was laid off in early September, but I know exactly why I was laid off, which I will now explain:

Since last December, I had been one of the many people assigned to design AOL 4.0 for Windows (AOL 4.0 beta, codenamed Casablanca). In the beginning, I was very proud of this task, until I found out the true cost of it. Things were going fine until about mid-February, when me and 2 of my colleagues started to suspect a problem, an unexplainable 'Privacy Invasion', with the new version. One of them, who is a master programmer, copied the finished portion of the new version (Then 'Build 52'), and took it home, and we spent nearly 2 weeks of sleepless nights examining and debugging the program, flipping it inside-out, and here is what we found.

Unlike all previous versions of America Online, version 4.0 puts something in your hard drive called a 'cookie' (AOL members click here for a definition). However, the cookie we found on Version 4.0 was far more treacherous than the simple Internet cookie. How would you like somebody looking at your entire hard drive, snooping through any (yes, any) piece of information on your hard drive. It could also read your password and log in information and store it deep in the program code. Well, all previous versions, whether you like it or not, have done this to a certain extent, but only with files you downloaded. As me and my colleagues discovered, with the new version, anytime you are signed on to AOL, any top AOL executive, any AOL worker, who has been sworn to secrecy regarding this feature, can go in to your hard drive and retrieve any piece of information that they so desire. Billing, download records, e-mail, directories, personal documents, programs, financial information, scanned images, etc. Better start keeping all those pictures on a floppy disk!

Figure 5.2. The AOL Cookie hoax used a personal style to create credibility.
Source: ciac.llnl.gov/ciac/ciachoaxes.html#aolcookie.

This is a totally disgusting violation of our rights, and your right to know as well. Since this is undoubtedly 'Top Secret' information that I am revealing, my life at AOL is pretty much over. After discovering this inform

attain, we started to inform a few other workers at America Online, so that we could get a large enough crew to stop this from happening to the millions of unfortunate and unsuspecting America Online members. This was in early August. One month later, all three of us were unemployed. We got together, and figured there was something we had to do to let the public know.

Unemployed, with one of us going through a divorce (me) and another who is about to undergo treatment for Cancer, our combined financial situation is not currently enough to release any sort or article. We attempted to create a web page on three different servers containing in-depth information on AOL 4.0, but all three were taken down within 2 days. We were running very low on time (4.0 is released early this winter), so we figured our last hope to reveal this madness before it effects the people was starting something similar to a chain letter, this letter you are reading. Please do the following, to help us expose AOL for who they really are, and to help us and yourself receive personal gratification for taking a stand for our freedom:

1. Forward this letter to as many people as you can (not just friends and family, as many as you can)!

2. Tell people who aren't on America Online in person, especially important people (Private Investigators, Government workers, City Council)

3. If the information about the new version isn't exposed by the time AOL is released early this winter, for your own protection, DON'T DOWNLOAD AOL 4.0 UNDER ANY CONDITION!!!

Thank you for reading and examining this information. Me and my colleagues hope that you will help us do the right thing in this situation.
Enjoy America Online (just kidding!)

Regards, A former AOL employee

Figure 5.2. Continued

```
PENPAL GREETINGS!

The PENPAL GREETINGS! hoax shown below appears to be an attempt
to kill an e-mail chain letter. This chain letter is a hoax because
reading an e-mail message does not execute a virus nor does it exe-
cute any attachments; therefore the Trojan horse must be self start-
ing. Aside from the fact that a program cannot start itself, the Trojan
horse would have to know about every different kind of e-mail pro-
gram to be able to forward copies of itself to other people.
Notice the three parts of a chain letter, which are easy to identify in
this example.

The Hook

    FYI!

    Subject: Virus Alert
    Importance: High
    If anyone receives mail entitled: PENPAL GREETINGS! please delete
    it WITHOUT reading it. Below is a little explanation of the message,
    and what it would do to your PC if you were to read the message. If
    you have any questions or concerns please contact SAF-IA Info Office
    on 697-5059.
```

Figure 5.3. The Penpal greetings chain letter.
Source: hoaxbusters.ciac.org/HBMalCode.shtml#aolcookie.

have a similar pattern. From the older printed letters to the newer
electronic kind, they all have three recognizable parts: a hook, a
threat, and a request."

By looking for these three parts in an email message, it's possible
to identify an electronic chain letter. The message cited in the epigraph to this chapter, for example, is a classic hoax chain letter. The
"hook" is the letter's appeal to our sympathy: a seven-year-old girl is
dying of cancer. The threat in this example is not overt, but it is
there: if you don't forward this message, you are denying Jessica's
dying wish and also denying needed funds to the American Cancer
Society. And the request is clear. Forward this note so the American
Cancer Society and corporate sponsors will contribute funds. Most

The Threat

This is a warning for all internet users - there is a dangerous virus propogating across the internet through an e-mail message entitled "PENPAL GREETINGS!".

DO NOT DOWNLOAD ANY MESSAGE ENTITLED "PENPAL GREETINGS!" This message appears to be a friendly letter asking you if you are interested in a penpal, but by the time you read this letter, it is too late. The "trojan horse" virus will have already infected the boot sector of your hard drive, destroying all of the data present. It is a self-replicating virus, and once the message is read, it will AUTOMATI-CALLY forward itself to anyone who's e-mail address is present in YOUR mailbox! This virus will DESTROY your hard drive, and holds the potential to DESTROY the hard drive of anyone whose mail is in your inbox, and who's mail is in their inbox, and so on. If this virus remains unchecked, it has the potential to do a great deal of DAMAGE to computer networks worldwide!!!!

Please, delete the message entitled "PENPAL GREETINGS!" as soon as you see it!

The Request

And pass this message along to all your friends and relatives, and the other readers of the newsgroups and mailing lists which you are on, so that they are not hurt by this dangerous virus!!!!

Figure 5.3. Continued

chain letters follow the same specific pattern: the hook is usually about a dying person, the threat is that you will be denying someone's last wishes, and the request is, in keeping with the features of speed and reach, to forward the note to as many people as you can. The CIAC offers another analysis of a chain letter (Figure 5.3).

Another way to identify a hoax chain letter is to look carefully at the header. By simply checking the email address of the supposed dying child in one chain letter (Figure 5.4), you can easily determine that the message is a hoax. If you try to connect to the Web site www.MayoHospital.health.com, you find that it is not a valid address. But the author of this message knew about the power of

These are a few new hoaxes that play upon the sympathy of people, and they are making their way around the world. The first chain letter has the subject "MAY HEAVEN LET THE LIGHT SHINE DOWN ON YOU" and claims that it is the dying wish of a young boy to have a chain letter go around the world forever. But look at the header. . . .

From: Anthony Parkin Parkin@MayoHospital.health.com
>>>>>Date: Wed. 17 Apr 1996 12:46:46 +0800
>>>>>To: [deleted: LG]
>>>>>Subject: My dying wish
This message is a forgery! "Anthony Parkin" posted from a FAKE ADDRESS! there isn't even a "MayoHospital.health.com"!

Figure 5.4. A chain letter that uses the Mayo Clinic's name and relies on people's desire to forward information quickly and without checking it first.
Source: www.nonprofit.net/hoax/catalog/chain_letters/chain_letters.htm.

speed: instead of carefully checking the source, most recipients of this message simply forward it to their friends. And by using the name of the respected Mayo Clinic, the author established immediate credibility, even though this note has nothing to do with the famous health care facility.

JOKES AND HUMOR

Jokes often act like chain letters. Your friend in Ohio comes across a funny anecdote and, inspired by the speed and reach of cyberspace, sends it to you and several hundred other friends. It's his way of reaching out and saying hello. You, in turn, pass it along to your mother, your sister, and anyone else who might like it. Why not? It takes only one click of the mouse to send it to everyone.

Unfortunately, these files, sometimes very long and often not really very funny, take up space on people's computers. They take time to download. And they don't really convey anything useful.

For many people, jokes and humor are a form of spam, which is the cyberspace term for junk email sent to huge lists of recipients. Spamming has the effect of the boy who cried wolf one too many times. When recipients see what appears to be a humorous message from someone who usually sends these, they delete the message without reading it. When an important message is sent, it can get deleted, too, just out of habit. In addition, one set of technical experts notes that "some recipients of large quantities of spam find themselves so over-whelmed with unwanted email that it is time-consuming or difficult for them to ferret out their desired correspondence" (Cranor and LaMacchia 1998). Some newer email programs actually have settings that can filter out junk email automatically.

VIRUSES

Viruses are real. These forms of software can do all sorts of nasty things to your computer. But because people do not understand how viruses work or how they are transmitted, they have become the perfect scare tactic for many hoax and chain email messages. In fact, viruses cannot be spread by simply reading an email message. They can be spread via attachments. The simplest way to determine what viruses are currently going around is to bookmark a few credible Web sites. The CIAC site and other good sources for this information are listed at the end of this book.

One observer has suggested that all forms of hoaxes and chain letters are "thought viruses" because they infect users and cause them to pass along the hoax letter to others! Describing the grand-father of them all, the "Good Times" hoax message, he sarcastically says: "Its [sic] for real. Its [sic] an opportunistic self-replicating email virus which tricks its host into replicating it, sometimes adding as many as 200,000 copies at a go. It works by finding hosts with defective parsing apparatus which prevents them from under-standing that a piece of email which says there is an email virus and then asking them to remail the message to all their friends is the virus itself" (Shirky 2000). This is a good point. Hastily passing along a hoax message before checking into it is wasteful and point-less, much like the spreading of a real computer virus.

Inaccurate Web Pages

Hoaxes and humor abound on the Internet, not only in the form of email messages but also on Web sites. Anyone with a computer, an

Internet connection, and a little bit of time to learn html coding or a Web authoring tool can create sophisticated Web pages. When everyone is a publisher, we end up with a vast world of information at our fingertips. But it is important to keep a careful eye out to judge the truthfulness, source, and credibility of what we see online. Extremist sites, for example, often masquerade as informative ones (see Chapter 3). In print publishing, and on television and radio news, information is screened by editors, reviewers, and fact-checkers. This feature, while it does not automatically lead to "truth" (after all, any newscast or publication has a particular slant), does provide steps along the way where information can be checked. On many Web pages, particularly those run by individuals, these gatekeepers are missing. But a Web site run by one person can have the look and feel of a site that belongs to a major news organization, and it can reach just as many people. The power of reach and the sophisticated visual tools make us believe in what we see.

An excellent example of a hoax, Web style, is a page about the city of Mankato, Minnesota (Figure 5.5). This site displays a photograph of a beach with a swimmer relaxing in the warm sun. It lures Web surfers to come and surf, literally, on the beaches of its lovely lakes:

> Mankato, Minnesota is truly a wonderland. Tucked into the Emerald Green Valley in Southern Minnesota, it is the hidden vacation Mecca of scores of knowing Midwesterners. Mankato has everything thanks to a freak of nature: the Farr/Sclare Fissure. This fissure in the earth's crust takes water seeping through the earth, heats it to well over 165 degrees, and sends it back up to the surface in steam pits and boil holes. The heat from these pits and holes heats the valley air to such an extent that the winter temperature in many Mankato neighborhoods has never dropped below a balmy 70 degrees!!!! Come enjoy our winters! Let's "Make It Mankato" !!

Trouble is, there is no such thing as the "Farr/Sclare Fissure." Mankato gets as cold as the rest of the state. Yet the site drew viewers from around the world, many of whom requested more information on lodging and travel. Soon the site had to include at the top of its

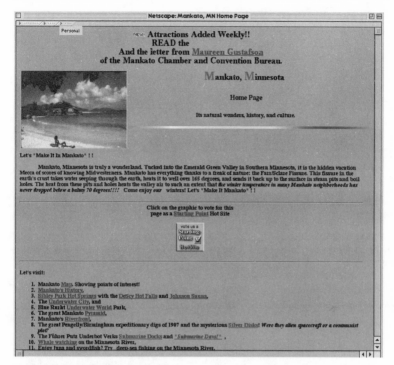

Figure 5.5. This lovely scene, inviting us to vacation in Mankato, is a spoof.
Source: www.lme.mankato.msus.edu/mankato/mankato.html.

page a link to a disclaimer informing Web surfers that Mankato was no place to surf the waves in December!

The Mankato Web page, a perfect example of how communication in cyberspace can be deceiving, is similar to the email hoaxes described earlier: it uses technical language (the "Farr/Sclare Fissure"; "takes water seeping through the earth, heats it to well over 165 degrees") and personal appeals to draw readers in. And unlike email, Web sites have the full power of textual, audio, and visual techniques. The photograph of the woman on the beach lends this Web hoax an additional element of credibility.

Evaluating Web Sites

One might wonder what harm there is in a site like the Mankato page. After all, a little humor can be a good thing, and this site is not extremist or angry. But with many people, including students, conducting most of their research on the Web, it is important to have the tools to separate hoax and humor from fact. Many educational institutions and libraries have begun to realize this and have created guidelines for helping people determine when a Web site is credible. Yet these numerous sets of guidelines can be confusing and inaccurate, and sometimes they offer conflicting information. In 1999–2000, a University of Minnesota undergraduate and I conducted a research study compiling these guidelines, with the goals of analyzing the guidelines and creating our own set. We examined 19 lists of criteria created primarily by colleges, universities, and high schools and identified several categories of criteria that can be used to judge Web sites.

AUTHORSHIP

All of the guides we studied stressed the importance of avoiding anonymous sites, and most urged that researchers look further to find the author's credentials and contact information. We agree that if you can determine the author of a site, you will have a better sense of its credibility.

CURRENTNESS

The currentness of a Web site's information was an important criterion in most of the guidelines, although this feature was expressed in a number of ways. Twelve of the sources suggested searching for the date of the site's last revision, and 13 stressed the importance of determining whether the information had recently been updated or took current research into account. We agree that in most cases, Web sites with more recent dates are probably more reliable. In some cases, however, information does not change much over time (as in, for example, a site listing Shakespeare's plays).

PURPOSE

Most sources suggested analyzing the site's intended audience. Indeed, 12 of the sources emphasized determining a site's purpose, evaluating whether it explains, informs, or persuades, and assessing its level of formality. If, for example, you are looking for a site that is intended for a college-educated audience with general knowledge about a topic, a site that is designed for specialists in that field will probably not be what you need.

URL

Nearly half of the guidelines considered a Web site's URL, or address, as a criterion for credibility. Some guidelines suggested that sites with addresses ending in ".net" may not be as credible as others, but this rule of thumb does not make much sense. While ".edu" sites are always educational institutions and thus may offer some hope for credibility, who is to say that ".com" sites, just by being commercial, are a better source than ".net" or ".org" sites? In addition, many ".edu" sites belong to students and may be personal home pages, not informational sites. Remember, however, that ".com" stands for "commercial," and on many commercial sites, the primary purpose may be to sell you something, not to educate you.

LINKS

The guidelines we examined presented a number of ideas about the credibility of links. Some sources said that Web sites should have relevant, workable links to support their ideas; if the links on a site do not work, this indicates that the site is not well maintained and therefore is perhaps not a good source of information. We agree that a credible site is one that works, but if only one or two of the links don't function, you should not discount the site entirely.

ACCURACY

Depending on the type of Web page, several features determine the page's accuracy. One major criterion (according to eight of the sources we examined) is appropriate citations for the information included. A credible Web site should indeed have accurate citations. Yet Web sites often reference other sites that share the original site's opinion, thus bolstering its viewpoint with the same view. It's important to determine not only whether a link is accurate but also whether it is a well-balanced source of information.

Five of the lists we examined suggest analyzing a Web page's design to determine the usability and professionalism of the site. This rule of thumb requires some scrutiny; the best-looking Web site does not mean the best information. It means only that the organization spent time and money to design a good site.

The credibility of a Web site, then, involves many factors. To be cyberliterate, we must be more than passive recipients of online information; we must assess whether a site is the most credible or appropriate for our needs. This is a skill that should be taught at all levels, from kindergarten through college.

What Motivates a Hoaxster or Jokester?

With all the misinformation around in cyberspace, you may ask yourself why it is that people spread hoaxes in the first place. There are many possible motives.

THE HACKER'S ETHOS
Long before your grandmother had an email address, computer programmers had developed a sort of personality cult. The thrill of watching a complicated piece of code run is part of what drives many software developers. Anyone who has spent even a little time writing code knows the feeling. You spend hours working out the details of a piece of software, then, with great anticipation, you press a key and watch it run. Although it's not fair to generalize, many computer programmers thrive on this feeling, and in the early days, when computer programming was still an esoteric sport, groups of programmers shared ideas over the Internet and reinforced this feeling. Tracy Kidder, in *The Soul of a New Machine* (1981), describes this ethos in relating how engineers at Data General in the late

1970s worked night and day, often propelled by a large amount of caffeine, to create their technological dream.

Some software developers, propelled by this high and the desire to watch their code float out across the wires, like a message in a bottle, will go beyond the fun of developing programs for a company and become full-scale hackers: people who develop code that runs across networks with the potential to wreak havoc on numerous systems. Hackers, often young and male, will explain when interviewed that theirs was an act of concern, because their piece of code actually exposed a hole in the various firewalls and security systems. But other motives have been observed in hackers. For example, often these people are shy and even anti-social, and they enjoy the power of hitting so many systems with such little effort. The anonymity offered by the Internet—a key feature in our discussion—helps hackers hide their true identities. They can sit back and watch the results of their efforts, as systems go down and powerful people in private industry and government jump in response. To some extent, the hacker ethos is like the ethos of flaming: you can hide behind the screen, sending out your digital fire and waiting for things to happen.

Initiating a hoax or chain letter is something like being a hacker. It is inspired by the same questions involving speed and reach: Where will the message land? How far will it circulate? Who will be foolish enough to believe it, and where will they take it? In some ways, it is similar to Mousetrap, a board game for kids that was popular in the 1970s: What happens when you release the little ball into the shoot? How many other mechanisms will it trigger? Although hoaxes and chain letters are not nearly as dangerous as the work of real hackers (who often distribute viruses or shut down systems), they are a variation on the same theme. In a way, hoaxes and chain letters give people a moment of power in a world where the power of individuals is rapidly being subsumed by corporate and government control.

PASS IT ON

Once a message has begun circulating, the seduction of speed and reach makes people pass things along before they think hard or

> Do not open Blue Mountain Cards until further notice.
> Virus has infiltrated their system. . .pass it on

Figure 5.6. Some hoax messages are short, but they still want you to spread the word. *Source:* www.stiller.com/oneline.htm.

do any research. Internet users seem to find this desire so seductive that some do not even taking the time to construct rhetorically complicated messages. Instead, they write simple one- or two-line messages (Figure 5.6).

In some cases, the instinct to pass it on reflects a sincere but misinformed desire to be helpful. As one group notes, "Hoax warnings are typically scare alerts started by malicious people—and passed on by innocent users who think they are helping the community by spreading the warning" (F-Secure Corporation 2000). In the days before email, many people had an aunt or best friend who liked to send newspaper clippings. And in a sense, having an email address is like being part of a global clipping service. Everyone can send you "important" news, and they can do it with very little effort. But unlike newspaper articles, what you get via the Internet has not been checked by an editor. It's information from the bottom up, and it's up to you to check it.

FEAR AND IGNORANCE OF TECHNOLOGY

Another reason why people forward these messages is that many Internet users are not technically sophisticated. In the "old" days of cyberspace (not so long ago), online citizens were usually affiliated with a technology company or a university, and they did not need much help to separate what was technically credible from what was simply a rumor. Most technical types know, for example, that it is not possible to get a virus from an email message (although you can get one from opening an attachment). Likewise, much of the Y2K hype that circulated via email during late 1999 was easy to sort out if you had a technical background but not so easy if you did not know, for example, that water systems don't rely on dates to provide homes with running water.

As the Internet increases its reach and becomes cheaper and more accessible, people representing a wider range of backgrounds will come online. When new users see a frightening message about the "Good Times" virus, they are likely to send it along, in good faith, to everyone they know.

MIMICRY AND PARODY

On the Internet, mimicry is a way of life. People learn to make Web pages not by remembering every single html tag imaginable; instead, they imitate what they see on another site, downloading the other page's source code and imitating it. Historically, the Internet has always been about sharing; early software engineers often passed their code over the network. And now, people see a message and feel compelled to send another, similar message. In this way, because there is so little gatekeeping or censorship on the Internet, everyone can become a publisher. Now that the genre of chain letters and hoaxes has become familiar, many people are trying out hoax writing. In fact, some people have begun combining hoaxes into one grand hoax narrative, as noted by the Stiller R News Web site (Figure 5.7).

You'll find mimicry and parody on the Web as well as on email. For almost any subject, and especially for almost any politician, you can locate not only the *official* Web site but also one or more parody sites (Figure 5.8). Sometimes these parody sites are hard to separate from the real thing, but in most cases the authors want to make it clear that they are making fun of someone, so after a bit of reading, it becomes evident that the parody site is just that. Like email messages that mimic some of the classic hoaxes, parodic Web sites use the format, language, and style of the original to create a derivative. If you are striving to be cyberliterate, you must learn to separate the parody sites from the official ones. It's not that you can't learn from the parody sites, because often they present a different perspective from the official line. But it's important to recognize these when you see them.

SR News: A Rerun: The Old Hoaxes Combined

The Old Hoaxes Return
We are now getting a lot of circulated hoaxes where someone has taken the older hoaxes and combined them in a single hoax warning message. This is really silly because anyone who has heard about any one of the individual hoaxes would most likely recognize that the combined hoax message is also a hoax. The originator(s) of these combined hoaxes probably think the combination sounds even more alarming than the individual hoaxes and will therefore be more widely circulated.

Please note that any time you get a warning message that mentions one of the hoaxes we cover on our list, you can assume the entire message is a hoax (or extremely misguided). These hoaxes often suggest you avoid messages or files with some particular title (such as "Undelivered Mail", "Join the Crew", etc.).

More and More Combinations
We're seeing more and more combinations. The following is an example of what is probably still the most widely distributed example of combined hoaxes. **If you see a message warning you about some threat and it includes any of the hoaxes covered on our hoax page, you can immediately disregard the message.**

The text of the most common form of combined hoax message begins with:

Subject: Virus!!!!!

Please read below!!!

WARNING!!!!!! If you receive an e-mail titled "JOIN THE CREW" DO NOT open it! It will erase EVERYTHING on your hard drive! Send this letter out to as many people you can. . . . . .this is a new virus and not many people know about it!

This information was received this morning from IBM, please share it with anyone that might access the Internet.

There's the typical hoax claim that this comes from some source of authority (IBM in this case) but this is the old standard Join the Crew Virus hoax which was just a minor ripoff of the original Good Times virus hoax. The hoax message then continues:

Figure 5.7. The mother of all hoaxes, illustrated by Stiller Research News.
Source: www.stiller.com/comb.htm.

Also, If anyone receives mail entitled: PENPAL GREETINGS! please delete it WITHOUT reading it!! This is a warning for all Internet users - there is a dangerous virus propagating across the Internet through an e-mail message entitled "PENPAL GREETINGS!".

DO NOT DOWNLOAD ANY MESSAGE ENTITLED "PENPAL GREETINGS"!!

This message appears to be a friendly letter asking you if you are interested in a penpal, but by the time you read this letter, it is too late. The trojan horse virus will have already infected the boot sector of your hard drive, destroying all of the data present. It is a self-replicating virus, and once the message is read, it will AUTOMATICALLY forward itself to anyone who's e-mail address is present in YOUR mailbox!

This virus will DESTROY your hard drive, and holds the potential to DESTROY the hard drive of anyone whose mail is in your inbox, and who's mail is in their inbox and so on. If this virus keeps getting passed, it has the potential to do a great deal of DAMAGE to computer networks worldwide!!!!

Please, delete the message entitled "PENPAL GREETINGS!" as soon as you see it! And pass this message along to all of your friends, relatives and the other readers of the newgroups and mailing lists which you are on so that they are not hurt by this dangerous virus!!!!

Please pass this along to everyone you know so this can be stopped. PASS THIS ON TO YOUR FRIENDS!!! WARNING!!!

This is the silly old PenPal hoax test which was (just like the Crew hoax above) merely yet another form of the original Good Times virus hoax. There are the typical requests to avoid a message with a specific title and the telltale request to forward the warning to all your friends. These are sure-fire signs of a hoax. Finally, the combined hoax warning terminates with a rehash of the old "Unable to Deliver" hoax. It ends:

There is a new virus going around in the last couple of days!!!

Figure 5.7. Continued

DO NOT open or even look at any mail that you get that says: "Returned or Unable to Deliver" This virus will attach itself to your computer components and render them useless. Immediately delete any mail items that says this. AOL has said this is a very dangerous virus, and there is NO remedy for it at this time. Please Be Careful, And forward to all your on-line friends A.S.A.P.

Forward this A.S.A.P. to every single person you know!!!!!!!!

There is (yet again!) the usual message to send this (so-called) warning to as many people as possible. **(This is a sure-fire indication that this is a hoax.)** Read our report on the <u>Undelivered Mail</u> virus hoax.

Figure 5.7. Continued

ANONYMITY

Although hoax and chain letters bring all features of cyberspace (speed, reach, and so on) into play, the feature of anonymity is especially worth noting. When no one can trace a message back to its author, the authors feel inspired to do things they otherwise might not. Not so very long ago, telephones did not come equipped with caller ID, and kids home sick from school often spent the day making prank phone calls: ordering a batch of pizzas for the neighbors or asking a stranger if she has Prince Albert in a can ("You do? Well, let him out!"). Today, caller ID makes prank calls almost impossible; even though you can block your phone number, some places (like pizza shops and mail-order houses) seem to be able to access your number anyway. But on the Internet, it's still easy to hide behind the screen of anonymity.

LACK OF GATEKEEPING

Right now, the Internet is a bottom-up medium: there is little gatekeeping of information, so ideas that would be reviewed before being published in other forums are readily posted across the world via the Internet. This lack of gatekeeping presents citizens of cyberspace with new challenges. On the one hand, there is so much in-

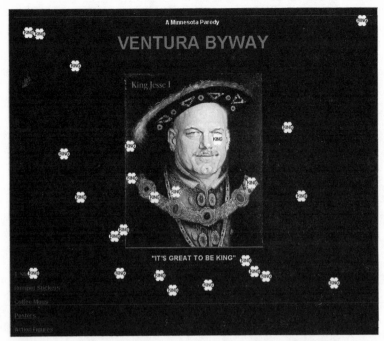

Figure 5.8. A parody of Minnesota Governor Jesse Ventura. Probably because the governor is known for having strong opinions and being somewhat controversial, he has inspired a long list of parody sites. You can view some at www.wcco.com/news/ventura/news-ventura-19991102–191054.html.
Source: www.pconline.com/~millcity/ventura1/ventura1.htm.

formation that you can find out almost anything. On the other hand, Internet users must be cautious. The power and playfulness of speed and reach invite us to forward messages quickly, but because so much of what we circulate has not been investigated, it's important to take a moment and check things out before passing them on.

LIFE IN PERPETUITY

A final possible motive for these messages and Web sites is that they give their authors a sense of living forever. Although your physical body will one day expire, your digital life can, in theory, exist indefinitely. The same is true for authors of print material, artists, musicians, scientists, and engineers, because once they have recorded, designed, or built their work, it has the potential to survive long after the artist has died. On the Internet, where everyone is an author and where one's audience is the entire globe, this sense of immortality may motivate people to send chain letters, which continually resurface. One chain letter takes this idea one step farther. This letter, supposedly from a dying child, asks people to "carry out my dying wish" by sending the message to "five people you know so I can live forever."

This motive may inspire people to create Web sites that commemorate a life, where visitors can read about the person, listen to a message, and watch a video. Although many of today's Web sites will be long gone in just a few years and most email messages get deleted after a while, some who wish to live forever continue to attempt to do so in digital space.

Internet Information versus Our Usual Sources

While Internet information abounds, it is clear that such information may come from a variety of sources, some credible, some questionable. Yet most people are used to getting their information from trusted news organizations (newspapers, television, radio), which operate in a way that is opposite that of the Internet. In traditional journalism, information follows a top-down model. Sources are checked and rechecked, stories are read by editors, and broadcasts are edited and spliced for length, sound, and content. But on the Internet, information is bottom-up. Anyone with a modem, a computer, and a bit of time can become a news source, because it is simple and cheap to set up a Web site and start publishing.

Take the case of Matt Drudge and the Drudge Report (www. drudgereport.com). This report started out as a gossip sheet for political happenings around Washington, D.C. Unlike a newspaper, it did not have any recognized editorial policy or gatekeeping. It was simply the work of one Matt Drudge, a former gift shop manager for

CBS with no experience in journalism but an ear for political happenings. His first postings were sent to a list of email addresses; later ones appeared on a Web site. Drudge's approach characterizes the open nature of information in cyberspace: bottom-up, no gatekeeping. It is up to readers to discern truth from rumor. Drudge gained national attention after he ran a story on 10 August 1997 about White House aide Sidney Blumenthal, which resulted in a libel suit; later, Drudge broke the Monica Lewinsky story. Mainstream journalists were alarmed by his style of reporting. In the opening remarks of his speech before the National Press Club on 2 June 1998, moderator Doug Harbrecht characterized the sentiments this way: "Drudge's methods are suspect in the eyes of most journalists. He moves with the speed of cyberspace, and critics charge he has no time to know his sources or check his facts. Like a channel catfish, he mucks through the hoaxes, conspiracies and half-truths posted on-line in pursuit of fodder for his website. That can have unpleasant consequences."

Drudge (1998) has responded that in many ways, he is similar to reporters of an earlier time, when anything was fair game and when citizens had more input into media coverage. He describes what he feels is a new, Internet-inspired model for journalism:

> We have entered an era vibrating with the din of small voices. Every citizen can be a reporter, can take on the powers that be. The difference between the Internet, television and radio, magazines, newspapers is the two-way communication. The Net gives as much voice to a 13-year-old computer geek as to a CEO or speaker of the House. We all become equal. . . .
> There won't be editors in the future with the Internet world, with citizen reporting just by the nature of it. That doesn't scare me. There's a notion that sticks and stones may break my bones, but words will kill me. I don't believe it. I get maligned every day on the news groups. I'm still standing. I still have a smile on my face.

Drudge's Web article (1998) was aptly titled "Anyone with a Modem Can Report on the World." Although this is an invigorating idea, cyberliterate citizens should note the implications: anyone with a modem can read this stuff. And because there is so little gate-keeping on the Internet, citizens need to become critical consumers of information.

The mainstream media, despite their adherence to a top-down model, are reshaping themselves to work within the new Internet model. Most television and radio stations, major networks, and print media now have Web sites, and these sites usually allow readers or listeners to interact with each other. In addition, journalists are frequently turning to Internet information as a source for a story, but often without a sense of the nature of such information. In the most famous case of this sort, seasoned journalist Pierre Salinger relied on an Internet source for his story that TWA Flight 800, which went down over Long Island Sound in July 1996, was hit by a missile. The source turned out to be nothing more than an Internet rumor. This clash of mainstream, old-guard media and unregulated, bottom-up Internet reporting will continue as the reach of the Internet expands.

Organizations Respond

Cyberliteracy is not important only for individuals; organizations also need to become conscious about the nature of information in cyberspace. Originally, many hoaxes and chain letters involved individual interests: purported files that would corrupt a personal computer's hard drive or kids who made dying requests. But soon, hoax mail began to involve companies and other organizations, and many were caught off guard.

In 1990, when Lotus Development Corporation discovered that messages about its forthcoming direct mail CD-ROM, Lotus Market-Place, were circulating over the Internet, company executives did not know how to interrupt the flow of inaccurate information. In those days, even computer companies were not adept at engaging information on the Internet. Today, however, companies often hire full-time employees and consulting firms to troll the crevices and canyons of cyberspace for what online participants are saying about their products and services. When any hint of misinformation develops, these teams are quick to respond.

FOR IMMEDIATE RELEASE
May 21, 1999
Release No. 45
E-MAIL RUMOR COMPLETELY UNTRUE
WASHINGTON—A completely false rumor concerning the U.S. Postal Service is being circulated on Internet e-mail. As a matter of fact, the Postal Service has learned that a similar hoax occurred recently in Canada concerning Canada Post.

The e-mail message claims that a "Congressman Schnell" has introduced "Bill 602P" to allow the federal govenment to impose a 5-cent surcharge on each e-mail message delivered over the Internet. The money would be collected by Internet Service Providers and then turned over to the Postal Service.

No such proposed legislation exists. In fact, no "Congressman Schnell" exists.

The U.S. Postal Service has no authority to surcharge e-mail messages sent over the Internet, nor would it support such legislation.

Figure 5.9. The post office hoax letter. *Source:* www.usps.gov.

In one example, the U.S. Postal Service was subject to an email hoax message, one that still rears its head from time to time. The message stated that a bill had been introduced in Congress authorizing the Postal Service to collect five cents on every email message sent in the United States. In response the Postal Service issued a press release both to media outlets and on its Web site (Figure 5.9).

With a little checking, those who circulated the message could have easily confirmed that it was a hoax before pressing "Send." First, as the press release notes, there is no Congressman Schnell. Second, the bill number is not valid. (Bills introduced into the House of Representatives begin with "H.R." and bills introduced into the Senate with "S.") This information would be easy for anyone living in the United States to verify, but for most people, the desire to pass along information outweighs any motive to check the information first.

Email Hoax Stories & Facts - from the Internet

1. Big companies don't do business via chain letter. Bill Gates is not giving you $1000, and Disney is not giving you a free vacation. There is no baby food
company issuing class-action checks. You can relax: there is no need to pass it on "just in case it's true."
Furthermore, just because someone said in the
message, four generations back, that "we checked it out and it's legit," does not actually make it true.

2. There is no kidney theft ring in New Orleans. No one is waking up in a bathtub full of ice, even if a friend of a friend swears it happened to their cousin. If
you are insistent on believing the kidney-theft ring stories, please see:
urbanlegends.tqn.com/library/weekly/aa062997.htm
"The National Kidney Foundation has repeatedly issued requests for actual victims of organ thieves to come forward and tell their stories. None have."
That's "none," as in "ZERO". Not even your friend's cousin.

3. Neiman Marcus doesn't really sell a $200 cookie recipe. And even if they do, we all have it. And even if you don't, you can get a copy at: www.bl.net/forward/cookie.html

4. There is no "Good Times" virus. In fact, you should never, ever, ever forward any email containing any virus warning. You can confim viruses at an actual
site of an actual company that actually deals with virii. Try: www.symantec.com/avcenter/hoax.html

5. If you still absolutely MUST forward that 10th-generation message from a friend, trim the headers showing everyone else who's received it over the last 6
months. It sure wouldn't hurt to ger rid of all the ">" that begin each line.

6. A composite of past popular e-mails—humor.

Figure 5.10. Some additional tips to guide you through hoax messages.
Source: email.calpoly.edu/emailfacts.html.

Toward Information Awareness

The lessons to be gained from this chapter all boil down to one main point: be aware. Once we know that speed, reach, and anonymity are key features of online communication, it becomes possible to take a critical stance when reacting to anything you find on the Internet. The tools (such as rhetorical analysis and critical viewing) presented in this chapter can help. Some additional tips, stated in a tongue-in-cheek manner, can also be useful for cyberliteracy (Figure 5.10). Along with these tips, you can take other actions to stay on top of things:

- Think before you post. Spreading simple hoaxes may seem harmless. But medical information, information about a scientific controversy, or hype about a politician's political life can have grave consequences.
- Don't start chain letters or hoaxes. Instead of using the Internet for wasteful messages or useless gossip, use it for promising things: educating children, teaching people about a new subject, or providing places for communities to gather.
- Teach new Internet users what to look for. If your cousin, mother, or friend gets a new Internet address and begins to send you chain letters or links to inaccurate Web sites, ask them to slow down and reflect before posting.

Being able to judge the quality of information we receive over the Internet is a big part of cyberliteracy. Another part is knowing what happens to information you don't see, such as the personal data you enter on a Web site. Who owns this data, and who can share it? The next chapter takes up the subjects of privacy and copyright.

Chapter 6
Privacy and Copyright
in Digital Space

[The Internet is a] George Orwellian version of a Cheers bar—a place where everybody knows your name, even if they shouldn't.
—Steve Case, Chief Executive Officer, America Online, speaking before the National Press Club (26 October 1998)

We impose government controls on techniques to protect privacy, where market-based solutions are preferable. And we leave privacy problems to the market, where government involvement is required.
—Marc Rotenberg, Director, Electronic Privacy Information Center, testifying before the House Judiciary Committee (26 March 1999)

For much of the twentieth century, people attended to the tasks of their daily lives without giving privacy and copyright much thought. Yet as the twenty-first century begins, these topics have become common ones for discussion, in large part because of Internet technologies. It is almost impossible to open a newspaper without encountering a story about privacy, or the lack thereof, on the Web. These stories raise such questions as whether it is safe to buy merchandise online when personal spending data will be collected and spread across cyberspace, not only by the companies that collect the data but potentially also by hackers who gain access to credit card information. And as countries begin to realize how wide-reaching these privacy concerns are, they start to wrestle with ways to protect privacy in the Internet age. Should governments regulate online privacy practices, or should industries regulate themselves? Given that the Internet has global reach but countries have conflicting laws and regulations about personal privacy, how do we address this question on a global level?

The topic of copyright, too, has been made explicit by the widespread use of the Internet. Most of us have gotten used to those little pieces of paper near a copy machine, which we often ignore, reminding us that copying may be a violation of copyright law. Yet cutting and pasting a selection from a Web site is still a novelty, and we do it without much thought. And like photocopying, reproducing or even downloading digital material may be a copyright infringement.

In educational settings, no one is really sure if articles can be legally posted to Web pages or if what used to count as plagiarism is really plagiarism anymore. In the corporate world, the desire to gather all possible information about a customer may overshadow important ethical concerns. In the home, creating a Web site that copies the basic style and format of another is not just a temptation but the way things are usually done. To be cyberliterate, then, Internet citizens need to understand the issues of privacy and copyright and to anticipate the changes that may come.

Privacy and the Internet

In the early twenty-first century, there is no escaping the rhetoric of privacy. In newspapers, we read about privacy and biotechnology: Who should own information about your DNA? Are medical identification numbers a good idea? We read about privacy, or the lack thereof, on the Web and wonder if it is safe to make purchases online when most sites collect and spread personal spending data. We live with increasingly sophisticated data collection technologies, such as supermarket check-out cards conveniently designed to clip onto your key chain and be scanned each time you make a purchase. The supermarket chains tout these technologies as ways to help you save money, but what they forget to tell you is that your supermarket and all its corporate affiliates, like Anna in *The King and I*, are interested in "getting to know you"—in matching your information with other demographic groups, and selling your information to other marketing services.

This scene is seductive, frightening, and confusing. It is seductive because media hype, our primary source of information on the issue, draws us into the discussion through scenarios that paint dark pictures of what is to come. Like Steve Case of America Online, many of us have come to believe that the Internet is a place where everyone can find out about us, even if we don't want them to. This idea is frightening, because we feel out of control. Who has our information? Who is watching us? What can we do about it? Privacy in cyberspace is confusing, because few of us understand privacy as a legal or political concept and thus do not know what our rights are, what is truly being done in cyberspace, and what is happening on the global stage. And it is confusing because our leaders are not taking effective action. As Marc Rotenberg says in the epigraph of this chapter, the government has taken a heavy hand on some privacy issues—mainly that of encryption software, which would let users control who sees their information. But when it comes to data collection and personal privacy in cyberspace, the federal government has defaulted to a laissez-faire model, letting ostensibly "neutral" market forces dictate how personal information should be used in the Information Age. Some state governments have begun to enact online privacy legislation, but this approach is piecemeal and not in synch with the global nature of the Internet, which spans boundaries and requires a more comprehensive approach to privacy.

In addition, Internet technologies challenge older rules about privacy, rules based on different hardware. In a case in Washington State, a judge determined that the privacy we should expect in regard to our Internet communication is different from what we expect and what the law says about the telephone. In most states, it is illegal to tape a phone conversation without obtaining permission. So when the police used transcripts of email messages and online chats, the defense argued that this evidence was obtained illegally, because no one asked permission to use these materials. But the judge decided that laws about taping telephone conversations do not apply to email or chat logs. She argued that when someone is using a computer, they are implicitly agreeing to have their information recorded, on the screen and on a hard drive (Kaplan 2000).

Few of today's Internet users give this idea—that their words may be used in contexts they never considered—much thought. A good guideline for cyberliteracy is that you should never post anything on the Internet, whether on a Web site or via email, that you would regret seeing in a different context.

Our concerns over privacy are not new. Definitions of what constitutes "public" and "private" are primary features of the U.S. Constitution; these discussions date back to the early days of the country and, ultimately, to English law. Specifically, U.S. citizens have been concerned about privacy in relation to most new technologies; the train, telegraph, telephone, radio, and television have all renegotiated our sense of public and private space. Tom Standage (1998, 110) explains how the telegraph, for example, raised privacy concerns, because unlike postal carriers who delivered letters in sealed envelopes, telegraph clerks could easily read a message at any point in its transmission. Particularly since the advent of the microcomputer, discussions of privacy have increased, with most focusing on surveillance technologies, echoing Shoshana Zuboff's (1988) concerns about an "information panopticon," where others can see everything you do but you have no idea who is watching or what they are recording.[1]

The cases of Lotus MarketPlace and the Clipper chip (Gurak 1997) provide early evidence of just how concerned people have been with personal privacy issues in relation to the computer. Both cases raised fears about "Big Brother," and both were widely protested by online activists. Since the time of these cases (1990 and 1994, respectively), other surveillance technologies, particularly those associated with the Internet, have been creating even greater causes for concern. Numerous surveys indicate that while people may not understand all of the intricacies of privacy law, they are concerned about what happens to their personal information. The Electronic Privacy Information Center (EPIC) cites just one of these studies, conducted by Forrester Research (www.forrester.com), which found that 67 percent of the people surveyed were very concerned or extremely concerned about online privacy, and an additional 24 percent were somewhat concerned (EPIC 1999a).[2] Other studies and informal surveys confirm this feeling: people are nervous about online privacy, but they don't know enough to make informed choices.

Watching You in the Background: The Myth of Anonymity

Much of this fear is valid, because these technologies do their work in the background. On the one hand, anonymity is a key feature of cyberspace, allowing users to connect but remain nameless, but on the other hand, new technologies are being designed every day that can look through the veil and watch users click and move about from screen to screen. Take the most recognized example: the cookie. A cookie is a file that a Web site sends to your computer and uses to track your whereabouts during your visit to that site. Cookies can also track information that identifies who you are and what Internet provider and even computer you logged in from. Different spins can be put on exactly what a "cookie" does. Take, for instance, Amazon.com's version: "'Cookies' are small pieces of information that are stored by your browser on your computer's hard drive. Our cookies do not contain any personally identifying information, but they do enable us to provide features such as 1-Click(sm) shopping and to store items in your shopping cart between visits. Most Web browsers automatically accept cookies, but you can usually change your browser to prevent that. Even without a cookie, you can still use most of the features in our store, including placing items in your shopping cart and purchasing them" (Amazon.com 2000). Amazon.com does a nice job of explaining its approach, but notice the perspective: cookies are your friends; they help you shop. Many sites provide even less information, and few Internet users even know about cookie technology or that they can change their "cookie preference" either to be notified each time a Web site sends a cookie or to refuse to accept cookies at all (Figure 6.1).

John Logie (1999) has argued that cookies might not be all that bad if their window messages were more accurate and informative. The message in Figure 6.1 tells me some information: the cookie will not be sent to other domains. But it should also tell me what the cookie will do: it will reside on my hard drive and store information

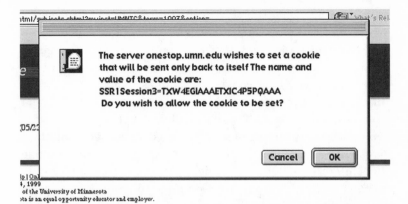

Figure 6.1. The University of Minnesota class-scheduling system sends cookies. With my preferences set to warn me before accepting a cookie, this is the screen I see first. If I choose "cancel," I won't receive a cookie, but I may have trouble registering. *Source:* onestop.umn.edu.

about what sites I visit, for example. In addition, many Web sites will not allow you to access certain features if your browser is set to turn off cookies. And if you set your browser to warn you before accepting cookies, you are often barraged with 10 or more windows requiring you to click "cancel" before you can even see the first page of a Web site. These sites seem to be saying "Turn off automatic cookies if you like, but we'll make it such a pain for you to use our site that ultimately you'll just give in." An alternative to giving in, from a cyberliterate perspective, is to write the company and complain about their use of cookies, or to find an alternate site that takes a better approach.

Other technologies are even more insidious about watching you. The Pentium III chip, for example, which runs many of today's personal computers, was originally designed to collect information about a computer user without that person ever knowing it. The chip was to contain a unique serial number that Web software would access to determine the identity of the computer. When the chip was first introduced, many privacy advocates were shocked that Intel, the chip manufacturer, did not provide a way for users to turn off this feature. Again, there are many ways of spinning the issue; Intel's version, as reported by the *New York Times,* was that this chip would "enhance the security of electronic commerce and guard against software piracy" (Clausing 1999). But this chip was even more problematic than cookies, because users did not know the chip was there. Eventually Pentium made this feature optional (and one can also download software to disable it), but the company did so only because of intense pressure and media coverage. Typically, a parody site, called "Big Brother Inside" (a play on the Intel theme "Intel Inside"), emerged to provide information about the chip.

Other privacy invasions come from the software side. RealNetworks' products (RealAudio, RealVideo) are the current standard used by most people to listen to radio and sound files and to watch video. When it was discovered that one of its products, RealJukeBox, was secretly tracking which sites users were visiting, several consumers sued the company, which quickly promised to release a "patch" that would let users opt out of being tracked. The very fact that Internet software developers continue to make products that spy on users is a real problem, because it means that each of us is required to be constantly on guard about our personal information. Meanwhile, it seems like most companies hope that people will just forget about the issue and inadvertently give in.

Ecommerce and Privacy

In the cases above, it is obvious that it's up to the user to opt out, request patches, turn off cookies, and ask companies not to sell or reuse personal information. Companies, by contrast, are free to do almost anything with the information they obtain. In the United States, there is no comprehensive policy to deal with personal privacy in general and with online privacy in particular. As with most issues in the United States having to do with corporate profits, privacy legislation reflects a laissez-faire model: leave companies alone, and they will do the right thing. But this piecemeal approach to privacy is problematic, because it favors large corporations over individuals and gives individuals little control over their own personal information. In addition, it puts the United States at odds with the privacy policies of many other countries. One place where the problems with U.S. privacy policy become readily apparent is in the wide-open playing field of ecommerce.

In a way, ecommerce is a retailer's dream. Companies can follow customers up and down the virtual aisles, watching what they look at, what they put in their shopping carts, and what they put back. Such virtual observation is better than any customer comment card. The corporate spin on this issue is that online customer information, gathered by permission or in the background, is a good thing, because it allows companies to provide you with better service. But because the use and sale of this information is barely regulated in the United States, there is another side to the story. Companies can sell this information, send you junk mail, and more. They can use your name and spending habits to make money without giving you anything in return and without your permission.

I often think of my father in these situations. When my dad bought a new car, he would always tell the salesperson not to put one of those stickers on the back, the kind that state the name and city where the car was purchased ("Carl's Buick and Subaru; Albany, New York"). Once a salesperson told him that the sticker was already in place, and my Dad said, "Well, you can leave it there if you deduct a thousand dollars from the cost of the car." The way he figured it, this was free advertising. Why shouldn't he be compensated for it? Likewise, all the personal information that you make available online is being used for the profit of that company and others. But we barely think to say no, especially because we have no idea what is being collected or how it is being used, and also because we in the United States have been raised with the laissez-faire model and don't often think to question it.

In an interesting twist, Amazon.com decided in the summer of 1999 not only to track your purchases but to link you with people who seemed to be like you, lived near you, or worked in your organization. These "purchase circles" surprised many shoppers and privacy activists. No one in particular had asked for these. And Amazon.com had certainly not asked its customers if it could use the data in this way. Yet its own privacy policy, posted on the Amazon.com Web site, was worded so that it allowed the company to do this. After some uproar, Amazon.com provided an "opt-out" policy that allows customers to reject having their data used in this manner. But once again, the burden is on the customer to know about this feature and take action to opt out.

As with much Internet technology, the purchase circle was designed without any discussion of individual privacy or the need for this feature. Instead of contacting citizens and asking for their input, our technology companies move full speed ahead with their approach, often just because they can. Let us not forget that when caller ID technology was introduced, consumers were not given a choice about whether they wanted their phone numbers broadcast or not. Only after much activism were phone companies forced to include the blocking feature.

What can we do to protect our personal data online? One suggestion has been to adopt an approach based on the European model, or at least to use this model as a point from which to begin modifying the scattered, invasive, and unregulated approach now used in the United States.

The European Data Directive and the U.S. Approach to Privacy

One commentator has called the American approach a "crazy quilt of narrowly drawn privacy laws" (Etzioni 1999), noting that privacy laws are usually drafted in response to specific situations; for example, the Video Privacy Protection Act was passed after a list of videos rented by Supreme Court nominee Robert Bork was made public. There are laws about who can access your driver's license number or how consumers can change mistakes on their credit reports. Yet a comprehensive approach to privacy is not part of the U.S. scene. In today's conservative political climate, when citizens and politicians alike seem distrustful of government rules (but trustful of the marketplace, for some reason), there is little impetus to create a broad approach to online privacy.

The U.S. approach is not practical in this time of widespread Internet communication. For one thing, these technologies present privacy issues far larger than ever before. The convergence of the

Internet, cable television, telephone systems, major media conglomerates, and banks present unparalleled opportunities for these companies to sort, sell, and use personal data in ways never before imagined.

In addition, the global nature of the Internet presents serious challenges to U.S. privacy policy. In the United States, barring any of the piecemeal legislation mentioned, anyone can collect any information they like and can resell it to other marketers. When you scan in your "customer discount card" at the grocery store, for example, you are giving out your name, address, and spending habits to this store and to anyone they care to sell this information to. In Europe, by contrast, companies must first ask permission to gather this information, then they must provide a mechanism for you to see and correct your information. In some European countries, information we consider standard, such as the phone numbers we dial each month, are never collected. A Swedish phone bill lists the total you owe, not the numbers you dialed.[3]

This conflict between the U.S. laissez-faire model and the European model is heightened in cyberspace. The growth of the Internet took place at the same time as the creation of the European Union (EU), and during this time, the EU developed the European Data Directive, which governs all EU members and states unequivocally that citizens have a right to their personal information. Doreen Starke-Meyerring and Kirk St.Amant (1999) at the University of Minnesota have analyzed the directive with an eye on the differences between U.S. and European approaches to privacy. They first note the stipulations of the EU directive, indicating

> that organizations gathering personal data on EU citizens must
> 1. identify themselves/their organization or company
> 2. identify the purpose for which they are collecting this personal data
> 3. identify who could possibly become a recipient of this data
> 4. state explicitly if questions concerning personal data are required or optional
> 5. explain explicitly what right the subject has to later access the data he or she gives the data collecting organization

Next, they discuss the first proposed U.S. approach to compliance with the EU directive. This attempt, called the Safe Harbor Principles, was designed to provide some compatibility with the EU directive, but Safe Harbor is not the law. It is instead a voluntary guideline for U.S. companies who wish to comply. As Starke-Meyerring and St.Amant note, this approach does not pack any punch: "If the enforcement mechanism has no legal way to make American companies comply with safe harbor, where is the incentive for such companies to actually adhere to the new data dissemination regulations? Thus, while the idea behind the Safe Harbor Principles is well intended, the means for executing that idea is greatly lacking and could potentially become a reason for the EU to reject the continued use of the Safe Harbor Principles."

The failed attempts at industry self-regulation have been noted. Industry regulation groups such as TRUSTe, which online companies can join and then display a seal of approval, are not adequate. In the RealJukeBox case noted earlier, RealJukeBox was in fact a member of TRUSTe, but the group did not investigate RealJukeBox even after the obvious privacy problems because of a minor technicality: "The TRUSTe license agreement only covers information collected from individuals over a website. TRUSTe claimed that since the information collection and transmission occurred through software downloaded at a site, there was in fact no violation of the license agreement" (EPIC Alert 1999).

Similarly, a study by EPIC examined 100 popular shopping sites on the Internet to see if the sites conformed to the "Fair Information Practices" (a set of principles, partially based on the law, that provide basic consumer privacy protection). The conclusions were startling: "We found that 18 of the top shopping sites did not display a privacy policy, 35 of the sites have profile-based advertisers operating on their pages, and 86 of the ecommerce operations use cookies. Not one of the companies adequately addressed all the elements of Fair Information Practices. We also found that the privacy policies available at many websites are typically confusing, incomplete, and inconsistent. We concluded that the current practices of the online industry provide little meaningful privacy protection for consumers" (EPIC 1999b).

This study confirms the observations of Starke-Meyerring and St.Amant, who maintain that the wide array of U.S. privacy policies on the Internet are confusing for users. They note the use of such phrases as "this policy may change from time to time so please check back periodically" and argue that consumers will spend only so much time rechecking the privacy policies of a Web site. They have also examined the language of policies on various Web sites, sampling 14 sites and concluding that few of these would stand up to the EU directive. They remark on the difference in tone between the U.S. sites and those a European citizen would encounter, observing that on U.S. sites "the option not to receive mail was couched as a generous gesture, using such statements as 'we *give* you options,' or 'we intend to *give* you *as much control as possible* over your personal information.' While the wording does not reflect any of the particular principles outlined in the EU Directive, it points to differences in basic assumptions: Who is giving what to whom? Or who is taking what from whom—with what right? According to the EU Directive, the individual would *have* these options and would have control over their own information. A policy could only *respect* these rights, but not *give* them to the individual" (Starke-Meyerring and St.Amant 1999; emphasis added). For many businesses, the EU directive is not viewed as a chance to examine U.S. privacy policy. In fact, the European approach makes many American companies defensive: "[The] European Union (EU) has issued an ultimatum regarding personal privacy: Play by our rules or don't play with our data" (IBM 2000).

We still have a long way to go before the global village is more than a cliché. Privacy policies in the United States, Europe, Canada, Japan, China, and elsewhere will continue to challenge us and invite a cyberliterate approach, one that requires online citizens to be aware, speak up, and take action when needed.

Can I Use This Clip Art? Copyright in the Digital Age

A second major legal and philosophical issue being challenged by emerging technologies is copyright. As it stands, the Internet promotes an open approach to information. It's common to cut

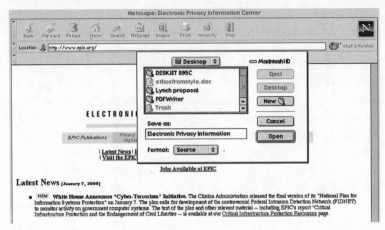

Figure 6.2. "Save as source." We take for granted the ability to save any Web site's source code, but this may not always be possible. It's not hard to imagine a time when a dialog box pops up and asks you to input your credit card information before you can save the html file. *Source:* Electronic Privacy Information Center, www.epic.org.

and paste from one email to another, link your Web site to someone else's, copy a graphic from a Web site, or import text from one site to another. This is no surprise given the history of the Internet, which started out as a space for sharing ideas, software, and research. The design of browsers, like Mosaic or Netscape, continued this trend: developers built in a feature to let you save the source code (the html file) for a Web site (Figure 6.2). From a commercial perspective, this may not make sense. This source code may have taken a team of people weeks to create, yet anyone with a browser can copy it. Why? Because it's the ethos of the Internet to share. Yet this ethos is challenging traditional notions of copyright.

Electronic technologies, especially those associated with the Internet, have created a confusing and challenging time for copyright policy. Standard practices in cyberspace—resending email messages; blending visual, textual, and audio material on Web pages; and copying and pasting information from a variety of sources—are often in violation of current copyright law. Although some lawyers believe that existing copyright law "seems to hold up rather well in this new digital world" (Cavazos and Morin 1994, 156), online practices defy traditional copyright, leading others to ask how much the law can protect against what has become common practice and what, as most readily admit, is inherent to the technology itself. For example, most email systems include the ability to forward material to others rapidly, and most Web browsers have easily accessible menu commands that allow simple downloading of sound, images, and even html code. In other words, "electronic media is a technology that does not support boundaries, either physical or conceptual" (Katsh 1995, 233).

Yet copyright law, based on the idea of physical property rights where boundaries are clear, is now up against the new terrain of cyberspace—sound, pictures, and texts that have multiple authors and are widely distributed from email message to Usenet newsgroup to Web page. The question, as Yale's Associate University Librarian Ann Okerson (1996) put it, is whether cyberspace is a "Wild West, where anyone can lay claim to anyone else's creations by scanning and uploading them or simply copying a few files" and therefore if the time has come to "dispense with copyright as we have known it" (81). Lawyers like Catherine Kirkman (1996) would reply that copyright is probably here to stay, because "if the past is any guide, we should expect technological advances to result in more copyright protection, not less" (14).[4]

Evidence supports Kirkman's claim. As more and more corporations discover the power and potential of doing business via the Internet, increased regulations and stronger protections in favor of intellectual property holders are sure to follow. Legislation that extends copyright by another 25 years (the "Sonny Bono" copyright act of 1998) strongly favors the copyright holder, not the public, and is an example of the trend toward a corporate paradigm, rather than a Wild West model, in cyberspace. Copyright legislation that favors large media conglomerates continues to be introduced. One of the first pieces, the National Information Infrastructure (NII) Copyright Protection Act of 1995 (HR 2441 and S 1284), was called a "wholesale giveaway" of the public's rights (Samuelson 1996) and would have considered a simple download of a Web page into RAM or the forwarding of an email message as a violation of copyright.[5] This exact bill was not passed, but new incarnations of it continue to be drafted.

In describing the electronic era, M. Ethan Katsh (1995) notes that "copyright is in a difficult and highly challenging period not simply because copying is rampant and enforcement is difficult, but because, even though it has not yet been widely recognized, the nature of our relationship with electronic information is vastly different from our relationship to print" (219). Yet I would argue that this relationship to electronic information has indeed been recognized, perhaps not widely, but by entertainment and media conglomerates who have much to gain or lose depending on how new copyright laws relate to electronic property. If this trend toward mega-mergers continues, students, educators, artists, and even these large media companies will find a vastly decreased amount of public-domain material from which they can draw, and in the end we will be sorely limited in our ability to use the vast amount of information that is available in electronic spaces.

One way out is for us to recognize that copyright was designed as a balance both to protect those who own the information and to allow uses of this information under what is called the doctrine of fair use. Fair use means that there are certain times when you can use information without requesting permission. The major points used to determine if your use is fair include the following:

- What is the purpose of the use? (Commercial or educational?)
- What is the nature of the copyrighted material? (Published or unpublished?)
- What is the amount or substantiality of the portion used?
- What will the effect of the use be on the value of the copyrighted material? (Patry 1985, vii)

Material that is used for educational purposes and that is based on excerpts of previously published material is generally considered fair. In addition, uses of material for parody and criticism are also covered by the fair use doctrine. For this book, I am using most of the images that I copied from Web pages for educational purposes and for the purpose of academic criticism. Thus, under fair use doctrine, I was not legally obligated to obtain permission to use these images (see the Appendix for more explanation of my copyright choices for this book).

In spite of the discrete look of this list, fair use is not a black-and-white issue, and courts often reflect vastly different interpretations of this doctrine. In recent times, the interpretation of fair use in the courts is becoming stricter. Martha Woodmansee and Peter Jaszi (1995) note this trend, indicating that "American judges have been interpreting copyright and 'fair use' in ways that restrict our freedom to use [unpublished material as sources] in our own [scholarly] writings" (775). In addition, the strong language included with many commercial products (such as those software licensing statements we never read as we tear through the shrinkwrap) tends to paint an unbalanced picture of copyright and fair use. As L. Ray Patterson and Stanley W. Lindberg (1991) argue, corporate entities now use what they call "baselessly exaggerated copyright notices" (such as the familiar phrase stating that "no part of this publication may be reproduced . . . ") to "promulgate guidelines that purport to implement [copyright law] but instead often constitute self-aggrandizement at the expense of public interest" (10). These licensing statements ignore the doctrine of fair use, making it seem as if *all* reproduction done without permission is a violation, when in fact many instances of reproduction are proper. Because the general public is not aware of the notion of "public" in terms of copyright, for many of us these statements tend to be our only encounters with this law, thus biasing our opinions and our practices concerning what we can and cannot use (Patterson and Lindberg 1991, 12).

We live, then, with a paradox. The Internet promotes open information, and fair use doctrine states that under certain conditions, it is not necessary to obtain permission. But all around us, through increasingly restrictive legislation and harshly worded licensing statements, we are being told that it's not OK to share. Even a concept so fundamental to the Web as the idea of linking to another Web site has come under the scrutiny of copyright law.

Cyberliteracy, Privacy, and Copyright

Cyberliteracy means more than just surfing the Internet and knowing how to click a few buttons. It means understanding your legal rights and paying attention to how the forces behind the technology of cyberspace are changing our social spaces. In terms of privacy and copyright, these changes are being driven by a laissez-faire, market-dominated model, and unless we participate in the decision making, the Internet of the future will be driven solely by corporate interests, not those of citizens.

Because new laws are being enacted constantly, it's important to keep up with the legislative action in your state and your country. As I write this, for example, Minnesota is debating privacy and data collection and considering new legislation that will protect consumers. Using the speed and reach of the Internet, it's easy to read about these debates and to voice your opinion to your elected officials. If you are a teacher, you can incorporate these discussions into your classrooms and student projects.

You can also take control of the technology and "toss your cookies," as John Logie says. Turn off the cookies in your browser preferences, and if some sites won't give you access without setting dozens of cookies that get sent around the globe, write to the site owner and voice your concerns.

Law professor and Internet scholar Lawrence Lessig (1999) promotes a technical approach to the problem. "Look to the code," he says; design systems that allow users to have control over their information, that "enable machine-to-machine negotiations about privacy so that individuals can instruct their machines about the privacy they want to protect" (163). How should this be done? He notes, accurately I believe, that the market is not the answer. Market forces would like even more access, not less, to personal data. He says, "Collective action must be taken to bend the architectures toward this goal, and collective action is just what politics is for. Laissez-faire will not cut it" (163).

And in the end, that is the truth. The market alone will not design a truly rich, collaborative, community-oriented Internet. Citizen action—by cyberliterate citizens—must balance the current trend toward a completely commercial Internet. For ecommerce is not entirely a bad thing. It is creating new models of consumer power and making shopping more efficient and focused. The next chapter takes us on a tour of the E-Mall.

Chapter 7
Shopping at
the E-Mall

In the Net Future, an infinite amount of information about customer desires and needs can be accumulated in real time. With the coming explosion in electronic commerce, that ability to capture customer information will drive demand to make greater use of the data being captured — and to do it quickly to keep up with the constant inflow of new data.

The combination of more information and more sophisticated use of it is about to give customers new and unprecedented power to get what they want, the way they want it, when they want it. Companies also will be faced with new capabilities to satisfy those needs and desires, before a customer is even aware of them.

— Chuck Martin (1999, 65)

While ecommerce can indeed be a wonderful tool, it is shortsighted in the extreme for some interests to treat the incredible creation that is the Internet as little more than a giant mail order catalog, with .com associated hype on seemingly every ad, billboard and commercial. . . . The Internet can be a fantastic tool to encourage the flow of ideas, information, and education, but it can also be used to track users' behaviors and invade individuals' privacy in manners that George Orwell never imagined in his 1984 world.

— People for Internet Responsibility (www.pfir.org)

On the Internet, you can buy almost anything—cars, books, CDs, software, clothing, kitchen products. Some Web shopping sites are friendly and neighborly. Others are designed to serve people who are looking for high-tech items like software or computers. This phenomenon—shopping at an electronic mall, not your neighborhood shops—is part of a bigger trend called ecommerce.

One of the largest ecommerce sites to date is Amazon.com, which sells books, CDs, videos, electronics, and more.

Like a traditional shopping mall, these sites invite you to visit, fill up a shopping cart, and use your credit cards. But unlike physical malls, e-malls let you do everything from home in the comfort of your own pajamas. Online shopping saves time, because instead of driving from store to store, you can surf until you find what you need. And you can customize your shopping experience to zero in on exactly what you are looking for. Do you hate walking through the housewares aisle to get to the camera department? No problem on the Web: just search for cameras, and there you are. Always find yourself behind that one annoying customer who selected the item without the price tag? On the Internet, you can avoid customers altogether. It's like having a store configured just for you. In some cases, you can avoid the store altogether and shop person-to-person, making bids on other people's stuff on sites like eBay. Or, with online services like Priceline.com, you can bid on items and services based on what *you* want to pay, not what the store wants to charge you. With a few simple mouse clicks, you can be on your way to a shopper's paradise.

Corporations—new ones like Priceline.com and traditional ones like General Motors—now have a major presence in cyberspace. This chapter examines the phenomenon of Internet shopping and raises questions about the increasing commercialization of the Internet. According to many analysts, online business revenue will reach into the trillions of dollars by the early twenty-first century. Ecommerce, driven by billions of dollars and massive advertising campaigns, is almost always presented as good, forward-thinking, and inevitable. We rarely stop to consider that ecommerce, like everything on the Internet, brings with it cause for concern. Here I look at online shopping from two perspectives—the positive and the problematic.

Ancient History: "No Commercial Advertising"

Only a few short years ago, this boom in ecommerce and the major corporate presence we now take for granted on the Internet would have been unimaginable. In fact, the very idea of using the

Internet for advertising was considered bad form, and anyone who tried to do so was roundly flamed for it. Take the case of two Arizona lawyers who in 1994 decided to explore the Internet's commercial potential. They sent advertisements for their legal services around the Internet; in particular, they were trying to solicit clients who might require their services in order to participate in an upcoming green card lottery (a green card is a U.S. document issued to non-citizens who want to work in the United States). Not long after the lawyers sent their note far and wide via email and mailing lists, they began to receive angry messages reprimanding them for using the Internet for such unabashed commercial purposes. One such note, reprinted in the *New York Times,* read: "When I first saw this notice, I thought, ah well, a kind-minded soul offering a useful service to aspiring US residents via the net. But your message keeps on appearing, in whatever group I read. Suppose, now, that every two-bit merchant follows your act. This thinly-veiled advertising contravenes the tenets of the Internet with respect to commercial promotions. NO COMMERCIAL ADVERTISING, if you please. Imagine what this vulnerable medium would look like if hundreds of thousands of merchants like you put up their free ads like yours. And you're LAWYERS! Educated parasites, if you ask me" (Lewis 1994).

The lawyers, new to the Internet, had committed two offenses. They had "spammed" the Internet (sent their message out broadly and without solicitation), and they had offered a commercial service. (Those lawyers went on to release a book on doing business on the Internet.) Yet in 1994, the Internet was viewed not as a place for commercial advertising but as a place for community, sharing, and public discourse.

Today there is no need to imagine what a commercial Internet would look like. Everyone with an address receives unsolicited commercial email, in large part because we have accepted that the commercial model is the one that will drive how the Internet grows and develops. No one expresses horror at the idea that you can get a free computer in exchange for letting advertisers display their ads twenty-four hours a day, and few people are alarmed if they receive a commercial email message or two in their daily batch of correspondence. On the Internet, ecommerce is growing faster than any public or non-commercial venture. Today the green card message would simply provoke a quick press of the "delete" key. We would certainly not stop to question the commercial side of cyberspace.

An important part of cyberliteracy, however, is questioning determinism. In this case, we need to ask if ecommerce and the commercialization of cyberspace was, in fact, inevitable. The answer is no. Until just a few years ago, the Internet was funded with public dollars from the National Science Foundation. When Congress decided not to renew these funds, we as a nation were making a choice about the philosophy of the Internet. Instead of continuing to fund part of the technology and carve out a portion that would be dedicated to non-commercial, public space (like public television or radio), we decided that the marketplace would be the best force to develop this new technology. But the marketplace is not neutral. It is driven by profit. A blend of both commercial *and* governmental forces might have given us a more balanced Internet, but what we have today is beginning to resemble one large shopping mall. How can we, as cyberliterate citizens, enjoy the benefits of the e-mall but seek other models to strike a balance in cyberspace?

Shopping at the E-Mall: The Good Stuff

I do not mean to imply that the nexus of the Internet and the marketplace has been a completely bad thing. On the contrary. Ecommerce is reshaping how we do business, and in many ways it is giving power to the consumer. The bottom-up model of information that has always been part of the Internet, combined with the technology's speed and reach, make companies more accountable and give consumers access to incredible amounts of information. The following are just some of the valuable features of the commercial side of the Internet.

COMPARISON SHOPPING

In many ways, traditional retailing is similar to traditional media organizations in that retailers are the gatekeepers of information. They have the knowledge and power when it comes to their products, and they can shape this information in any way they choose. If you go to the store and try comparing the features of one clock radio, say, with several others, you find that the display card lists some features for one radio and different features for another. In a discount store, it's up to the customer to figure things out. In a more specialized outlet, such as an electronics store, customers turn to the salesperson for help, which can be a dangerous game, especially if that person is paid on commission. And even if the salesperson is particularly honest and helpful, he or she is only one source of information.

The Internet, land of speed and reach, is just the opposite. The bottom-up model of information in cyberspace means that anyone can broadcast whatever they have to say about a product. For anything you want to purchase, you can now find customer reviews, lists of dealer costs, and other sources of information. Some sites offer to take on the task of comparison shopping for you. And the information that you find is not just from your local discount store or friendly salesperson or even a few colleagues at work. It's from everyone, everywhere. Customers can review products and read each other's reviews, too.

I recently began shopping for a new car. Car dealerships are probably the most notorious culprits when it comes to withholding information about how much the car "really" costs. But on the Internet, I was able to locate several dozen sites that gave me dealer prices, safety records, customer comments, and more. In response to the Internet's bottom-up approach, car dealerships are changing. Many participate in Web auto-purchasing services, which allow customers to request prices and even purchase cars over the Internet. Still others are training their sales staff how to work with the new, informed generation of car shoppers. When I finally decide on a car, I can go to the dealer knowing exactly what I'll pay and what extras I want. Or I can order my car right over the Web, and my only interaction with the dealer will be when I pick it up. In general, online shopping gives customers more control.

CONVENIENCE

Shopping in the physical world is not always fun, especially if you are looking for an item that is carried by a range of stores in different parts of town. Driving, parking, and hoofing it through store after store can get tiring, and it takes a great deal of time. In one day, if you are lucky, you may be able to visit four or five stores. But on the Internet, unless your modem is having a really bad day, you can usually venture through at least ten times as many Web sites, gathering information and comparing what you find. In some cases, consumers will actually make the purchase online, too. Sometimes, people find that it's worth paying extra to be able to stay away from the shopping mall. One reporter, citing a study by ActivMedia Research, notes that "convenience and quality, not price, are the major motivators for online grocery buyers" (Cox 2000). If you've got the money, this is a great option.

INFORMATION ANY PLACE AND ANY TIME

When our clothes dryer stopped working, we called and arranged for a repair service to come to the house the next morning (there are still some things you can't do on the Internet). That night, I began to wonder what new dryers cost. If the repair charge was going to be close to the cost of a new one, then it might be time to replace my 14-year-old dryer. It was late—stores were closed—and the most recent issue of *Consumer Reports* (to which I subscribe) to review dryers was more than a year old. But it did gave me a sense of the repair record for certain brands. Now, what did these cost here in my market? A quick trip to the Best Buy Web site gave me a remarkable amount of information.

When you seek information on the Internet, it does not matter what time it is or where you are located. The Best Buy store in my city closes around nine in the evening, and I would have had to drive there, but online Best Buy was open and resided on my screen in my house. I easily found the dryers, located the brand I liked, got a price, and began exploring details. I learned all about "auto dry" and other features. My repair bill the next day turned out to be small, and I did not replace the dryer. But had I needed to, I knew exactly what I wanted. On the Internet, place and time do not impede access to information.

CREATE YOUR OWN JEEP

The Best Buy site was full of information, but a dryer is still a dryer, and there were only so many features I could check out. On

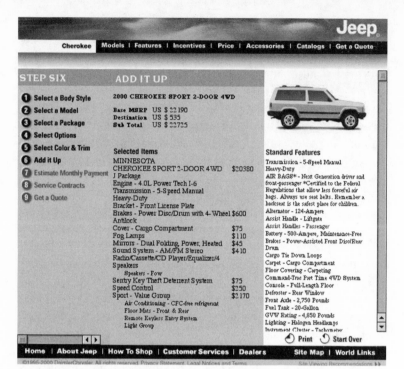

Figure 7.1. The Jeep Web site lets you build your own vehicle right down to color, options, and wheel covers. *Source:* www.jeep.com.

other sites, you can create your own custom product, as I discovered one cold day here in Minnesota. I began to think about trading in my six-year-old hatchback for a more snow-worthy vehicle, and when I decided to investigate the Jeep Cherokee, it was easy to do so online. I quickly found myself learning everything I'd ever wanted to know about Jeeps. In addition, I was able to build my own car, which was customized with the features I wanted and visibly updated on the screen each time I made a change (Figure 7.1).

Many sites let you build your own product in this manner. Although you could potentially do this at the dealership, too, if you do it from home there is no pressure. Because I don't accept cookies on my browser, the folks at Jeep did not know my identity. And unlike some sites, this one did not ask me to enter personal information before it let me in.

If It's All So Good, Why Complain?

You'd think that my Best Buy and Jeep experiences would be enough to make me come up short on any critique of ecommerce. After all, online shopping is giving us more information and more choices. Speed and reach, combined with a bottom-up organizational style and the ability to be anonymous (if you take cookie precautions and watch what you type on a Web site), create new potential for consumer power at the e-mall. So what are the negative consequences of this side of cyberspace?

THE CHANGING PLACE OF PUBLIC SPACE

Ecommerce further reduces our already shrinking public spaces, because it takes something that was public (the Internet, funded by public dollars) and creates an almost entirely commercial model. We don't often stop to consider that malls, virtual or physical, are not public spaces. They are privately held commercial sites where companies, not citizens, make the rules. Two brief stories illustrate how we tend to conflate private commercial space with public space.

When I was about 12 years old, my local Girl Scout troop decided to raise funds by holding a car wash. We made flyers advertising our event, contacted the local fire department for use of a water source, and then, early one morning, set up our supplies and hung large signs around the parking lot of a local mall, where we had decided to hold our event. After we washed one or two cars, a large Cadillac pulled up, and a stern-looking man came over to us. He did not want his car washed; rather, he was the owner of the mall property and wanted to know why we had not sought permission to use his space. We were taken aback, because we viewed the mall as a public place and had simply assumed that it was ours to use.

A similar event took place at one of Minnesota's famous cultural icons, the Mall of America. Large groups of teenagers had been hanging out at the mall, disturbing shop owners and shoppers. The mall management decided to make a rule: no unaccompanied children under the age of 18 on weekends. Some citizens and many young people were angered, and their comments in the local news media reflected an assumption that the mall was somehow *their* space. After all, it was the Mall of *America;* its very name suggests a public place where Americans, individual and free, can meet, mingle, and (of course) shop.

At one time, the Internet, too, was felt to be public space. Today, however, there are few, if any, skirmishes over public versus private space on the Internet. Instead of mingling with each other in public places—real (like a town square) or virtual (like a Web site for community news)—shoppers can now meet at commercial sites like Amazon.com or eBay. Regardless of how much these sites have absorbed from the bottom-up, speedy, and wide-reaching Internet, they are still commercial spaces, and their job is to sell things.

TWO HUNDRED CHANNELS OF HOME SHOPPING

If the focus on ecommerce continues to outweigh other motives and types of Web ventures, our notions of what is public and what constitutes public space—and the public spaces we have access to—will give way even more than they have already. Cyberliteracy requires us to think of visions of the Internet that invite public, noncommercial gatherings. Otherwise, the Internet will go the way of cable television, which originally held great promise for public access broadcasting and even electronic voting. Now, by the same laissez-faire model that dominates in cyberspace, cable television has become little more than hundreds of channels of home shopping (either directly, through home shopping networks, or indirectly, through commercial channels that seem to show more advertising than show).

We need to be especially aware of this lesson in today's environment, where elected officials seem to dislike anything with the word "public" in front of it. Attacks on public radio and television, arts funding, and the like are often premised on the idea that commercial ventures will give us the best outcomes. Several senators who favor cutting funding for public television, for example, seem convinced that we no longer need such funding in light of the wonderful educational shows on such cable channels as the Arts and Entertainment network (A&E) or the History Channel. While these channels do produce some fine programs, they do not compare to what is produced for public television, in part because commercial channels are always connected to profit, while public channels are more connected to ideas and quality. If we do not push for some public space and public funding for the Internet, we will end up with a technology rich in potential but used almost solely for selling things.

CUSTOMERS AS DATA

As one writer observes, the Internet's original ethos is affecting how we shop online. "The Internet," he writes, "is haunted by its own promise: the liberation of information. Typically, this promise is a strange hybrid of 60's progressive libertarianism and 90's aggressive venture capitalism. The slogan 'information wants to be free' still shapes the dynamics of on-line content consumption and production" (Stalder 1999). And free information on cars, dryers, and clock radios is a good thing, because it helps consumers get a clearer picture of what they want and need in a product.

In the beginning, when traditional retailers met up with cyberspace, they could not figure out how anyone would make money on the Internet. How, they puzzled, can a company make money in a place where information is supposed to be free but where high-quality, regularly updated Web sites are expensive to set up and maintain? What is the business model for this space? At first, many tried their traditional tactics, asking people to register, subscribe, and otherwise pay a fee. But when Internet users encountered fee-based sites, so at odds with the ethos of free information, they simply consulted other sites until they found a free page.

Suddenly, it seemed, businesses realized the trick, and it lay in the strength of community, enhanced by speed and reach, to bring together like-minded people in the same location. A Web site was a marketer's dream, so long as the site could capture information about those who visited and somehow get them to return. If you built it, they would click, and if they stayed there, you would suddenly have access to more customers than you ever could have imagined. And these were not just any old customers, the type that wander aimlessly in your store to kill time while their spouse picks out a pair of shoes. These are folks who want to be on your site and who found it because they need something.

The "if you build it" model of ecommerce immediately led to an increase in data privacy problems in the United States, because the incentive for companies to build expensive Web sites was to capture information about who visited the site. Because U.S. privacy laws say little about what companies can do with this data, the boom in ecommerce has heightened problems with personal privacy and data collection, and our lawmakers seem reluctant to mess with the marketplace enough to address this issue (see Chapter 6).

For many, privacy is not a problem at all. For Chuck Martin (1999), as quoted in the epigraph to this chapter, customers *become data,* and this feature is a benefit, not a concern, because "more information and more sophisticated use of it is about to give customers new and unprecedented power to get what they want." Never mind that the more sophisticated the use of your personal data, the more you are giving away for free and the less control you have over who knows your spending habits, computer type, income, and interests. Moreover, your personal information is often gathered in ways you don't know about (like the Pentium III chip) or used in ways far wider reaching than you may have imagined: "Because of the capacity of technology and the Internet to process and manipulate information, there is considerable value and competitive advantage in exploiting personal information. In unregulated free markets the interests of individuals are invariably overwhelmed by commercial considerations. While most information on the Internet is free, personal information retains value both to individuals and commercial interests. Unfortunately a black market in personal information has emerged on the Internet" (Bambury 1998). So far, even cyberliterate citizens can do very little to stop this trend. Still, it is important to be aware of how your personal data is being used before you begin interacting on a Web site, and it is important to contact local and national representatives to express your opinion on privacy and other legislation.

The online auction site eBay receives much attention because it draws on the community, people-to-people feel of the early Internet and uses (some would say exploits) this feature to create a successful site where people bid against each other on items they want to purchase. Chapter 3 describes the kind of wired, edgy feelings that result from too much time online, and nowhere is this more evident than in the bidding frenzies on eBay (Figure 7.2). People have described the anxious feeling of waiting for an auction to close, sitting

Figure 7.2. This cartoon by Stephen Kroninger, and others like it, characterize the downside of life on eBay. *Source:* Illustration accompanying James Gleick, "Stop me before I shop again," *New Yorker* (24 May 1999): 42. Courtesy of Stephen Kroninger.

poised and ready to enter another bid, and getting angry when they are not the highest bidder. Some have described their encounters on eBay as addictive because, driven by speed, they continue to bid on items they do not need and sometimes cannot afford. And now you can even use software packages to track your bids, allowing you to manage your online auctioning experience more easily but also hooking you in more deeply.

In addition, when we come to expect the speed of an online shopping experience, we may get even angrier when shopping in physical, face-to-face stores. I experienced this feeling one day while trying to purchase an inexpensive CD case at a local electronics store. The line was too long, there were only two cashiers, and the person in front of me was having credit card troubles. I began to think that if I had ordered the case online, it would have shown up at my office without all of this bother. Of course, my annoyance was somewhat misplaced, because the next day, when I tried to order some disks online, the server went down. But logic does not always prevail when it comes to emotions, and many people who shop on-line are reporting that the perceived slowness of shopping at a real mall makes them angry and impatient.

QUANTITY DOES NOT EQUAL QUALITY

Just because the Internet offers a lot of consumer information does not mean that the information is all equally valid. In fact, we are often swayed by Web pages that look and feel "real" and truthful but in fact are not (see Chapter 5). Some have speculated that the postings you find on a Web site do not represent a cross section of that population and may in fact be skewed toward people who have had serious complaints or problems. For example, on Web sites or newsgroups dedicated to health-related issues, only people who are the most ill or have the most severe reactions to a particular procedure or form of medication may be represented. Similarly, people who post messages on Web sites about, let's say, cars, may be those who have had trouble with a certain model, even if that model has a good track record overall. Cyberliteracy, then, requires a critical eye when it comes to judging information.

As ecommerce becomes the dominant model, a broader question comes to mind: Do we want to shop for everything? What about education, for example? Chapter 8 examines the phenomenon of distance education in more detail, but for now, it's useful to consider the relationship between thinking of the Internet as one big shopping mall and thinking of education in this same manner. Partly in response to the rise of the Internet and individualist trends in the workplace (like telecommuting), colleges and universities have been rushing to jump on the bandwagon of distance education.

Some schools are doing this with caution, evaluating the relationships between learning and technology. But others are simply putting as many courses as possible on the Web, hoping to attract the tuition dollars of thousands of students who otherwise would never come to campus, and to do this without the added expense of more classrooms or faculty. One critic of this trend calls these universities "digital diploma mills" (Noble 1999), while others take a deterministic attitude, much as people do about the loss of personal privacy: You can't stop progress, so what else can you do but give in?

Efforts at distance education vary, and I am not condemning all of them. But cyberliteracy asks us to consider the implications of this trend. When "students" become "customers," they begin to think of education as a *quid pro quo* relationship. On Amazon.com or any other commercial site, when you order a book or other item, you expect to get it in the mail a few days later. In a distance education setting, students may bring the same attitudes to the relationship: I order some education, and I expect to get what I paid for. Although students do deserve a well-organized, professionally managed class for their tuition dollars, this line of thinking may go too far: if students do not agree with the professor's opinions or pedagogical decisions, they may feel that they did not get what they paid for. Or students may think that distance education is a one-way transaction, like ordering a book: I order a book, and it's up to the company to make sure that it arrives, that I am satisfied, and so on. A learning experience is not like this, because it requires active participation from the student as well. Once a colleague of mine received an email message from a student in an online course. The student indicated that she had not realized that the deadlines for assignments were going to be taken so seriously! In a traditional class, this would not be questioned. But online, expectations are shaped in part by the ecommerce, consumer-to-company model, not the dialogic, collaborative model of student to professor.

TRUST AND SECURITY

We are still a long way from full financial security on the Internet, because it was not designed with ecommerce in mind. The Internet, connected across a vast network of computers in different countries, is not linear and not hierarchical. Thus, unlike more secure systems such as those associated with traditional, non-Internet banking, information on the Internet is still subject to hacking and other online mischief. In addition, software for Internet banking and financial applications are still in the early stages and are often not tested adequately before they are rushed to the screen. In one case, an online bank (X.com) that touted how easily it allowed you to move your money turned out to have major problems when it became apparent that anyone who knew your account number and bank routing information could also transfer your money (Markoff 2000). And the global reach of the Internet gives greater cause for concern, as when a hacker collected the names and credit card numbers from shoppers on a CD site and then tried to ransom these back to the company for a mere hundred thousand dollars. Apparently, the hacker was traced to somewhere in Russia, and no one knows for sure if he still has the credit card list or how he plans to use it.

ACCESS

Finally, not everyone can be part of the boom of ecommerce, because not everyone has access to the Internet. And because online shopping requires consumers to use credit cards, people with bad credit are also left out. Finally, because so much of the Internet is focusing on the commercial side, those without money, computers, or credit cards are at an even greater risk of being left on the sidelines than they ever were before. While I may be able to walk into the Jeep dealer and get my Jeep for 2 percent above invoice plus dealer costs on the options (because I had access to the Web), many others will not have this bargaining power and will end up paying too much—and these are the people who can least afford to do so.

Striking a Balance with the Dot.coms

Ecommerce is the main theme of the Internet boom (although recently, investors have discovered that good online businesses actually need a business plan!). And it does indeed bring some benefits. It offers great opportunities for consumers and is changing retailers, even the most rigid, like car dealers. In addition, the dollars being spent on ecommerce sites are helping create innovations in Web technology, innovations that spill over into other parts of the Web. But the swing toward a commercial Internet comes at the expense of public spaces and individual privacy. In an age in which legislators seem to bristle at the thought of government intervention, we probably cannot look for any help in that regard; in fact, a U.S. Commerce Department report titled "The Emerging Digital Economy" (1998) states in no uncertain terms that "where possible, rules should result from private collective action, not government regulation."

You can, however, practice cyberliteracy by doing what you can to balance the trend. For example, try to support local business at the same time that you enjoy the virtual marketplace. Be aware of the consequences of an entirely commercial Internet, and visit or start sites that do things besides sell: sites that enhance your local community, provide useful information, or offer a place for people to debate or get involved in discussions about the Internet. One project worth investigating is the Internet2, a new, high-speed Internet partially supported by public funds and designed to give researchers and universities access to more powerful processing power. Most states have at least one university involved in this project.

Although eBay and other online auctions promote themselves as being people-to-people, these sites are quickly becoming rather traditional commercial ventures. Instead of always using the big commercial sites, try connecting with people one-on-one via discussion lists and chat sites. When I decided to buy a Palm Pilot, for example, I found a used one from a person in Pennsylvania via a newsgroup. We exchanged email, talked briefly on the phone, then I sent him a check and he sent me the Palm. We still correspond from time to time!

You can also use the power of speed and reach to protest sites that ask for too much personal information but don't provide any statements about their privacy policies. If enough people sent email to just one of these sites, we'd quickly see a change in how they conducted business.

Finally, we can enact cyberliteracy by paying attention to those things that are best done in real life and separating our time on the Internet from time we could be spending offline, with friends or in our own neighborhoods. This is the subject of Chapter 8.

CHAPTER 8
THINK GLOBALLY,
EAT LOCALLY

Click, click through cyberspace; this is the new architectural promenade.
—William J. Mitchell (1995, 24)

We do not need electronic neighborhoods; we need geophysical
neighborhoods in all their integrity.
—Stephen Doheny-Farina (1996, xi)

Several years ago, I was on my annual vacation to the East
Coast ("out East," as they say here in Minnesota), staying with family
along the Connecticut shoreline. One day I took a break from the
sun and surf to drive north through Connecticut into the college
town of Northampton, Massachusetts. I had been away from Minnesota for more than a week, and I was desperate to find an Internet
connection, despite my earlier resolve *not* to read email for the entire vacation. After a visit with friends and a quick lunch, I began to
roam the city in search of a computer hooked up to the Internet.
First I tried the public library, but its computers allowed only limited
access to Web pages. Next I tried seeing if one of the computer labs
at Smith College might let me, a fellow academic, connect, but unfortunately their labs had just closed. Then someone told me about
"JavaNet," a café that combined real java, as in coffee, with computers and Internet connections. I soon found the place, and after paying my fee and connecting, I started happily working through more
than a hundred messages.

One message was from a good friend back in Minneapolis who,
coincidentally, used to live in Northampton. I replied to her email
and also noted where I was writing from, and I got an immediate reply. We chatted electronically back and forth, and then I began to re-

alize that I was getting hungry. So I sent my friend a message and asked where I should go to eat. As I was waiting for my reply, I over-heard two JavaNet employees behind me talking about a recent trip to Minnesota. An apt illustration of reach and speed, I noted. My friend quickly wrote back with a restaurant and menu suggestion. I turned to the clerks and asked, "Can you tell me where [such-and-such a restaurant] is? My friend in Minnesota just told me to eat dinner there." They laughed and pointed me down the street. I thanked my friend via email and logged off.

My friend on the other end of the Ethernet connection was as present as the two JavaNet clerks, and it felt as if I had been living in multiple worlds at the same time—me in my U of M T-shirt, the clerks talking about Minnesota, me in Northampton, my friend who used to live there giving me directions to dinner. But in the end, I could not get a meal from a Web site. I had to log off, get up, and leave the JavaNet café. Just down the street I found the Chinese restaurant, ordered the tofu with three kinds of mushrooms, and forced my now expanded sense of self back into real life so I could eat dinner.

No matter how much we work and play in cyberspace, we don't really live there, and we can't eat there, either. As Phil Agre (1998) has argued, "Cyberspace . . . does not exist. The Internet does exist, and so do a lot of other technologies, [but] neither the technolo-gies nor the changes are well described as the creation of a distinct, separate, autonomous pseudo-place that could reasonably be called 'cyberspace.'" Others, such as Stephen Doheny-Farina (quoted in the epigraph to this chapter), make similar arguments, proposing that too much time in virtual space is often spent at the expense of our physical spaces, like neighborhoods and homes. Yet observers like William Mitchell, an architecture professor at MIT (also quoted in an epigraph), point out that cyberspace is in fact the new public space, a virtual yet very real place where more and more of us go to hang out.

I agree with both points of view. Like Mitchell, I believe that on-line space is rapidly becoming a significant place where we debate, shop, and interact. But like Doheny-Farina, I believe that it is essen-tial to our health and well-being—physically, politically, and emotionally—to understand that we are still material beings with physical needs and desires, and that online technologies can never change this fact. As the little voice on my Macintosh computer likes to say, we are still "carbon-based life forms." In this final chapter, I emphasize the importance of physical space and the human body and suggest that while cyberliterate citizens should embrace the positive features of Internet communication, they should also consider the physical limitations of these technologies and the importance of the body, our material conditions, and our working environments. In other words, cyberliteracy includes an awareness of when to use digital technologies and when to interact with the physical world. Agre goes on to argue that "the concept of cyberspace is destructive because it draws our attention away from the most consequential effects of the adoption of distributed information technologies. It focuses our attention on unrepresentative cases, it interferes with our attempts to conceptualize the material and institutional context in which online interactions occur, and it makes us less likely to ask many important questions. Not only that, but the cyberspace ideology makes a vast number of predictions, the great majority of which are turning out to be 180 degrees the opposite of the truth" (1998).

We need to be careful how we assess the barrage of predictions and hype about the Internet. Being online brings with it opportunities for great things and troublesome ones, too. The consequences of what we do on the Internet resound in our physical world, and as the world becomes more and more wired, it will be increasingly critical for people to step back and recognize how the virtual affects the physical.

There Is Place, and Then Again, There Is Place

We use the metaphor of place to talk about the Internet, saying things like "I *went* to that Web site today" or "Let's *go* online." But we never really *go* anywhere. We sit in our chairs and interact with images, sounds, and text, and we feel as if we are going somewhere. To some extent, these feelings of being someplace in cyberspace are valid, because cyberspace, unlike television, is more than a one-way channel of communication. It is a place where our minds travel—a conceptual place—and if we want to feel like it's a real place, too, that can be fine as long as we remember to live the bulk of our lives in the real world. But sometimes, cyberspace happenings are conflated with real ones, and the results can be alarming.

A story known to many Internet denizens illustrates this confusion. It's often called the story of the virtual rape, and the main character is one Mr. Bungle, a persona on LambdaMOO (a real-time chat space run by the Xerox Palo Alto Research Center). Mr. Bungle, relying on anonymity and the ability to quickly come and go from MOO sessions, used some interesting programming tricks to make other characters on the MOO experience "virtual rapes" via strange puppet characters who would accost the other players. The episode was later described by Julian Dibble (1993) and published in the *Village Voice;* at one point, Dibble summarized it this way: "Which is all just to say that, to the extent that Mr. Bungle's assault happened in real life at all, it happened as a sort of Punch-and-Judy show, in which the puppets and the scenery were made of nothing more substantial than digital code and snippets of creative writing. The puppeteer behind Bungle, as it happened, was a young man logging in to the MOO from a New York University computer."

Dibble's commentary raises an important question: Was this really rape? Can virtual characters experience anything as horrific as an actual rape? The characters who were attacked on the screen were understandably upset, but to give this experience the same attention as should be given to the hundreds of women (and men, too) who experience real rape is simply not right. In the end, the people who were subjected to Mr. Bungle's programming skills and wordplay could simply log off and go back to their normal lives. Real rape victims never can.

Physicality Rules

The moral of this story and others like it is clear: our real bodies do not live online. And when it comes right down to it, what happens to our real bodies takes priority. Physicality, in the end, is the big rule. Physicality rules.

Yet our reliance on electronic technologies, from ATMs to telephones to the Internet, often keeps us separated from the harsh realities of the physical world. Every so often, however, a natural disaster reminds us that we are not our cyberspace identities. In January 2000, for example, the southern United States was blasted with record-breaking winter weather. Raleigh, North Carolina, received more than 20 inches of snow. My sister, who lives in Raleigh, had phone service, and she could send email as much as she liked. But she could not get out of her driveway because it and her entire neighborhood were not plowed, and even when she could get out, she could not get food because people were hoarding things. Cyberspace is many things, but it is not real space. In times of disaster, we are people who need to keep warm, eat, and sleep. And we cannot do these things via the keyboard and the screen.

Over the past 10 years, many scholars and commentators have begun to talk about the notion that we are becoming cyborgs: beings who are part human and part machine. They often cite as evidence such things as implantable medical devices (pacemakers or artificial joints, for example) or technologies like virtual reality, which let you interact with a computer system and feel as if you are in another world. Books like Donna Haraway's *Modest-Witness@ Second-Millennium.FemaleMan-Meets-OncoMouse* (1997) illustrate how the line between human and machine is blurring. She (and other scholars who examine the nexus of body and machine) note that among other things, gender becomes more complicated in virtual space; Allucquere Rosanne Stone (1992), for example, recounts the story of Joan (see Chapter 4) to illustrate wh̄ ᵔhe describes as "the collapse of the boundaries between the social and technological, biology and machine, natural and artificial that are part" of our postmodern world (85). Yet she goes on to point out that "no matter how virtual the subject may become, there is always a body attached" (111).

In the end, physicality makes the rules. If you get the flu, you will not have the energy to go online and spend hours chatting with your friends. You will be forced to ground yourself in the physical until you are well again. And it is your real neighbors who are close enough to drive you to the hospital if you need it.

Local Communities

Online space changes how we define and interact with the physical world, and one concept that has received much attention has been the idea of online community, which was described early on in book format by Howard Rheingold (1993). Many debates have focused on whether our clusters of common interest on newsgroups and the Web really count as community. Doheny-Farina (1996) raises the concern that while we may know people on the Internet on a first-name basis (or so we assume, even though one never can be sure who's on the other end of an email message), we are increasingly losing touch with our real neighbors. He maintains that we need to focus on our physical communities, or else we will find ourselves in a world where people barely know their own neighbors.

One approach to using the Internet and staying in touch with our local communities is the community network movement. Community networks (sometimes provided at no cost and called Freenets) sprang up in the early 1990s as a way to make communities stronger by linking them together via the Internet. Neighbors can read about local events, find out library hours, and chat with each other via their neighborhood networks. And most community networks maintain their connection to the real world in other ways, too, because they connect people to physical neighborhoods and communities (Figure 8.1).

Community networks are a useful way to blend the virtual with the physical. Yet sometimes we reach for technology when a far simpler act, like a knock on the door or a quick phone call, would suffice. I observed this disconnect in 1996 when I participated in the Apple Design Project at the University of Minnesota, a collaborative effort of the Department of Rhetoric and the Department of Architecture sponsored by Apple Computer. The theme was community, and our teams of students were to design and prototype a device that related to the theme. Several interesting projects resulted, but one that caught my attention was a small screen device, much like a lightweight laptop computer, designed specifically for the local neighborhood of Valentine Hills. This "community appliance" would allow neighbors to look up community events, find babysit-

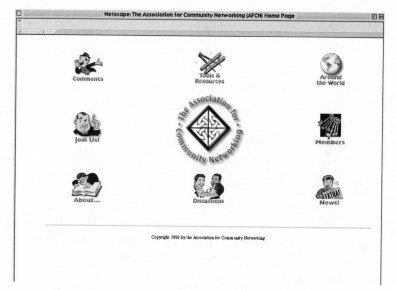

Figure 8.1. The Association for Community Networking offers links to community networks around the world. *Source:* www.afcn.net.

ters, and leave messages for each other. While the students' work was ambitious and creative, it struck me that it might be simpler for people to walk to each other's homes or make a phone call.

Another feature of online community that has negative consequences for real-life community is that online, if you don't like someone or don't like the conversation, you can simply log off or find another site. In real life, you can't disconnect. You need to learn to live with that person next door who owns a loud motorcycle, or with the family down the street who start their mower at eight in the morning. Instead of logging off, you might have to go over to their house and have a conversation. Living too long in the virtual, where it's easy to escape, makes you unable to live with difference.

Internet Fatigue and Internet Addiction

Even when the Internet is harnessed to strengthen local community, it is a technology that, in large doses, is not good for the body.

Although I always have known it, it has taken me this entire book to truly realize that even I need to take a break from cyberspace. I had always intended to write a final chapter about physicality and why we need to strike a balance between time spent online and time spent in our physical, grounded, local spaces. I had many arguments planned, but the one I did not count on was my very own body. Tonight, for example, it is approaching one in the morning, which is nothing new for me, as I regularly work late. But after several long days at the computer, I notice tonight that my body does not feel right. My brain feels tired, and although I have excellent vision, my eyes are getting sick of looking at the screen.

When I went into the kitchen to get a drink of water, I had an insight into what it really means to take a break from the Internet. It doesn't just mean getting up and walking away. It also means leaving behind the ways cyberspace makes you feel and think. The intensity of the screen and the seductive quality of type behind the glass make our bodies and brains function in ways they should not have to endure for long. The human body was meant to move about, breathe deeply, and stare off into the distance. The fatigue that accompanies long hours online is of a special sort, because it beckons you to stay there. And it may be increasing as a new generation of kids become "mouse potatoes," spending hours and hours indoors at the computer.

We're seeing more and more people haunted by Internet fatigue and other physical symptoms of being too connected for too long: carpal tunnel syndrome, bad backs, stiff necks, and even bad tempers. Maybe part of being a cyborg means walking around with a wrist brace, worn from too many hours of typing at the keyboard. Cyberliteracy includes taking breaks in order to stay healthy and exercise all parts of the body, not just the fingers and eye muscles.

Why do people stay online for so many long hours if it hurts? One theory is that there is such a thing as Internet addiction. I received an email message from a reporter working on just such a story (Figure 8.2). If he could have reached her, the reporter would have enjoyed speaking with Sherry Turkle. In *Life on the Screen* (1995), she studied undergraduates who spent hours and hours each day online; one student even noted that for him, RL (real life) was just another window.

Professor Gurak:

I'm a reporter form the Star Trib. A— P— in communications gave me your name. I'm doing a story on the phenomenon of computer/computer game addiction. I've interviewed people obsessed with the latest compulsion, a game called Everquest, dubbed "Evercrack," and some psychologists who have "intervened" in cases of "addiction." I'd be interested in talking to you about the issue. I've left messages on your office machine. Unfortunately, my deadline is Friday morning.

Please call if you can help.

J— T—

Figure 8.2. An email message from a Minneapolis Star Tribune reporter writing a story on computer addiction. *Source:* Laura Gurak.

Is cyberspace addictive? Several people think so. A site devoted to online addiction, run by psychologist Kimberly Young, author of *Caught in the Net* (2000), provides this definition:

> Internet Addiction is a broad term covering a wide variety of behaviors and impulse-control problems. It is important to understand that there are five specific types of Internet addiction:
>
> 1. Cybersexual Addiction (addictions to adult chat rooms or cyberporn).
> 2. Cyber-relationship Addiction (online friendships made in chat rooms, MUDs, or newsgroups that replace real-life friends and family, this also includes the issue of cyberaffairs).
> 3. Net Compulsions (compulsive online gambling, online auction addiction, and obsessive online trading).
> 4. Information Overload (compulsive web surfing or database searches).
> 5. Computer Addiction (obsessive computer game-playing or to programming aspects of computer science, mostly a problem among men, children, and teenagers).

The site then offers the following checklist:

> How can you tell if you are addicted? Here are some typical warning signs:
> 1. Do you feel preoccupied with the Internet (think about previous on-line activity or anticipate next on-line session)?
> 2. Do you feel the need to use the Internet with increasing amounts of time in order to achieve satisfaction?
> 3. Have you repeatedly made unsuccessful efforts to control, cut back, or stop Internet use?
> 4. Do you feel restless, moody, depressed, or irritable when attempting to cut down or stop Internet use?
> 5. Do you stay on-line longer than originally intended?
> 6. Have you jeopardized or risked the loss of significant relationship, job, educational or career opportunity because of the Internet?
> 7. Have you lied to family members, therapist, or others to conceal the extent of involvement with the Internet?
> 8. Do you use the Internet as a way of escaping from problems or of relieving a dysphoric mood (e.g., feelings of helplessness, guilt, anxiety, depression)? (Center for On-Line Addiction 1999)

If you can answer five or more questions affirmatively, then you may suffer from Internet addiction. But notice what they advise you to do: "If you fear that you may be addicted, we invite you to take our Internet Addiction Test. If you need immediate help, please contact our *Virtual Clinic*" (emphasis added). Yikes! A virtual clinic. This seems like only more cause for addiction. But perhaps once people make the step toward the clinic, they can move out of their addictive behavior long enough to realize that they need help.

Ecommerce and Physical Objects

Ecommerce, the biggest point of interest on the Internet these past few years, is anything but virtual. In Chapter 7, I described my interactions with two Web sites: the Best Buy site, which helped me learn about the features and costs of clothes dryers, and the Jeep site, which helped me create a customized car. I spent time on these sites not because I wanted to have a virtual experience of a dryer, but because I needed something in the physical world. Ecommerce is very much linked to the world of bodies and things, and not just because these sites are about items we want to purchase. Online shopping is ultimately rooted in real places, real books, and real people. I, like many others, was reminded of this fact when I tried calling Amazon.com on Thursday, 2 December 1999. No one was able to answer phones, because employees could not get to work. All of downtown Seattle had been shut down because of the protests over the meeting of the World Trade Organization. Ah yes, I thought. The physical meets the virtual.

The design of many ecommerce sites also has consequences for physical community. Until recently, shopping involved going into what some Internet types call "meat space," which is to say physical space, where people ("meat") mingle, eat, shop, and browse. But on many ecommerce sites, you never need encounter a person at all. You can surf around, find what you need, buy it, and log off. These sites heighten our sense of individualism at the expense of community. And even sites such as eBay, which are designed so that consumers can meet each other and exchange email or chat about things they have in common, cannot replace the experience of greeting people at a flea market on a summer afternoon. The consequence of speed and reach on ecommerce sites may be a fractured, fragmented sense of community.

Finally, the sheer quantity of consumer information on the Web can be wonderful, but it can also lead to exhaustion. I have a friend who will spend entire days reading and tabulating Web-based product reviews before she makes a purchase. She learns a lot, but she always seems pretty bleary-eyed after it all is over.

Distance Education

Speaking of being bleary-eyed, what would it be like to take all your college courses over the Internet? Besides the obvious problems with fatigue, eye strain, wrist strain, and the like, the trend toward distance education raises other issues of consequence for our physical lives.

The richest form of communication has always been face-to-face. Humans can communicate so much with their bodies. Vocal expressions, eye contact, and gesture constitute the best way to add meaning to what is being said. Friends may say, for example, "That hat looks great," but from their eyes, or by the way they are turned away from you, you can tell that they are just trying to make you feel good about a really terrible hat. Teaching relies on the same cues, and for thousands of years, students have learned by interacting—in the physical world—with other students and instructors.

David Noble notes that much of the current language about distance education echoes what was said almost one hundred years ago when correspondence schools were on the rise. According to his analysis, the physical settings of classroom and lecture hall are cast as negative by those who promote learning from your own home: "The rhetoric of the correspondence education movement a century ago was almost identical to that of the current distance education movement. Anytime, anywhere education (they didn't yet use the word 'asynchronous') accessible to anyone from home or workplace, advance at your own pace, profit from personalized, one-on-one contact with your instructor, avoid the crowded classroom and boring lecture hall" (Noble 1999).

If we are not careful about how far we go with distance education, we will sell ourselves out of the best type of learning there is: person to person. Yet the trend is strong toward a system of learning that emphasizes students as customers, turns schools into businesses, and—like the ecommerce models described in Chapter 7—elevates individualism over community. "Go to school?" asks one deterministic Internet speculator. "No, school will go to you in the Net Future—if you're motivated to learn. New technologies will create classrooms in which the students may be in 100 different locations, all different from that of the teacher. Whether in colleges or corporations, whether used to gain a degree or new technical skills, online education will become an increasingly popular way to help students and workers get the education they need to remain competitive in a rapidly changing world" (Martin 1999, 149).

Maybe this is true, and maybe it is not. It all depends on how much we value the richness of being together with each other in person. Much of what we learn in a classroom is how to get along with people who hold opinions we don't agree with. Online, you can log off or go out of the room if you don't like the discussion. Or you can send a flame or be ruder than you might be face to face. In a real classroom, you must face people in the flesh, and you must learn to disagree in a way that can be spirited but that also must be reasoned, civil, and respectful.

Not all distance education is negative. Many universities are acknowledging that students may appreciate this approach as a flexible component of their degree plan. But the thoughtful places are considering how to strike a balance, so that a degree involves some distance work but also some time in classes. Also, some schools are realizing that in order to do distance education well, it is important to develop methods to find out what works and what doesn't. (Ann Hill Duin of Iowa State University, for example, has developed a rubric for analyzing the effectiveness and appropriateness of distance education modules.)

In the fall of 1994, two other faculty (from different institutions) and I used the Diversity University MOO to conduct what we called a graduate "colloquium" on the topic of "rhetoric, community, and cyberspace." Earlier that year, we sent notice of the colloquium to several major graduate programs in rhetoric and composition and selected participants on the basis of their background and interests from applicants who responded to our notice. The participants were 14 graduate students, most of them Ph.D. students from the Midwest and Northeast, plus ourselves. That fall we read an article or section of a book each week for ten weeks and met for an hour on Thursday evenings to discuss the readings. One of us logged the discussions (captured the text of it) and sent the logs to all participants after each evening's discussion (see Zappen, Gurak, and Doheny-Farina 1997).

Because we were geographically so spread out, it would have

been impossible to conduct this colloquium without the Internet. The colloquium was not offered for credit (although some students signed up for independent study credits at their local institutions), so students who participated did so because they wanted to enhance their local educational experience. Thus we blended the physical with the virtual. And at the next academic conference where we all were in attendance, we all got together for a beer. Think globally, eat and drink locally.

Cyberspace Meets Outer Space

There are other ways for virtual space to meet up with the space we live in, the space that has consequences for our existence and our future. One of my favorites is the SETI at home project, which provides a nexus for some of the most profound and exciting aspects of the Internet (Figure 8.3). This project, based at the University of California at Berkeley, uses the reach of the Internet to harness individual computing power in an effort to do something beyond the individual: to analyze data collected with the Arecibo

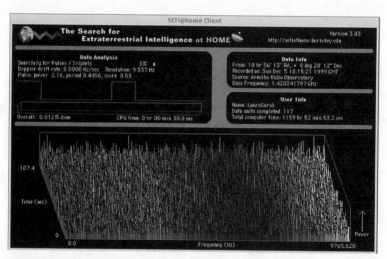

Figure 8.3. The SETI at home project reaches out across the Internet in search of life on other planets. *Source:* setiathome.ssl.berkeley.edu.

Radio Telescope, in Puerto Rico, for patterns that may indicate a sign of intelligent life. This site captures the Internet's excitement, because it reaches out to lots of computers on the desktops of regular people all over the world, allows all of us (not just scientists and researchers) to be a part of this exciting project, and reminds us that it's the physical that matters and that outer space holds new adventures and possibilities to excite our imagination. A site like this reminds us of the importance of physical space while presenting itself in cyberspace.

Cyberliteracy as Awareness and Balance

Although it's fun to talk about cyberspace as place, we reside in the physical world. We thus need to strike a balance in our wired lives. On the one hand, the power and potential of the Internet are vast, and many of the changes we are experiencing—in everything from shopping to falling in love to reading and writing—are exciting. On the other hand, there is no free lunch. Technologies have consequences, and the Internet is no exception. To be cyberliterate, we must be alert to the ways in which the Internet is changing our connection to our physical lives. And in doing so, we must make choices about what sort of activities are appropriate for cyberspace and what sort are better experienced in the physical world. Although there is no free lunch, there is still real lunch, which you just can't eat on the Internet.

In this book I take an eclectic approach, based in rhetorical criticism, qualitative content analysis, and academic criticism. My use of "key terms," though eclectic, is not anecdotal. It will strike rhetoric scholars as a somewhat Burkean treatment of the subject. Rhetorician Kenneth Burke (1973) felt that a critic could learn about the motivating forces behind a situation by using a method that he labeled "cluster analysis." To perform this sort of analysis, the first step is to "select the key terms or the most important terms used in the rhetorical artifact" (Foss 1989, 386). Then, by examining the dominant terms in any situation, critics "make a reasoned case for the consistencies of the parts and the whole, that is, for how the terms fit the apparent situation" (Brock 1989, 187). By gathering what I observe to be the dominant terms on the rhetorical landscape, I offer an interpretation of what we need to consider for a cyberliteracy—an interpretation that is based on years of observing, participating in, and criticizing the social features of cyberspace.

My views on the Internet are based on the specific moment in time I chose to do my analysis. As a reflective critic, I recognize that, as one set of scholars have noted, "criticism can and should only seek momentary interpretative closure in such a way as to remain open to further interpretation" (Brock 1989, 190).

Another important point about being a rhetorical critic is that criticism "is an inherently ethical activity, for future actions can be affected by the work of a critic" (Brock, Scott, and Chesebro 1989, 13). As such, I take my shaping of this book, and of what I call cyberliteracy, very seriously, and hope that it contributes to ongoing discussions on the social sides of cyberspace.

On Copyright and Fair Use
This book is an act of criticism. It is inspired by my own view of the Internet and by the wide range of research that I have read, conducted, and collaborated on for more than 10 years. As an act of criticism, my use of such material as Web pages, email messages, and magazine or newspaper clip-

pings constitutes fair use under U.S. copyright law. Academic criticism has long been covered by fair use standards, and in this age of the Internet, where information appears to be free but where large corporate entities are trying to strengthen their grip on copyright, it is imperative that scholars exercise fair use to its fullest extent.

Besides criticism, fair use is usually based on the following four factors:

- What is the purpose of the use? (Commercial or educational?)
- What is the nature of the copyrighted material? (Published or un-published?)
- What is the amount or substantiality of the portion used?
- What will the effect of the use be on the value of the copyrighted material? (Patry 1985, vii)

My use of the material in this book, along with its purpose for scholarly criticism, is educational, based on previously published material, uses only the amount needed to make the point, and does not have any negative impact on the value of the original. (If anything, the examples used in this book bring positive value to the original by pointing readers to these sources.)

I thus have made the choice to obtain written permissions only on items that were more of an embellishment to my narrative than an item used for overt criticism. Also, I have not obtained permission to use Web pages. For one, the Web pages contained herein are used for criticism. In addition, when a person or organization makes a Web site available to the world, that person or organization knows full well that the resulting Web page will be uploaded onto thousands of computer screens, linked to by other Web sites, and printed out on desktop laser printers. None of these uses require written permission, and a book, especially an act of criticism, is hardly different.

Out of respect for the privacy of individuals, I have deleted any real names or email addresses in the messages I cite. In addition, I provide full citations for the Web pages and images contained herein.

All online information (Web pages, email messages, mailing-list postings) is reproduced as it appeared during the period October 1999–June 2000. Unless otherwise noted, spelling errors and unusual typography (all capitals, for example) have been retained.

CHAPTER 1: CYBERLITERACY

1. Tyner (1998) characterizes current scholarship on literacy as research that values "literacy as discourse" (28), meaning, I presume, all discourse.

2. Welch (1999, 119–120) cites African American and Native American rhetoric as just two examples of significant oral traditions and later illustrates with a Native American myth. See Welch 1999 for a concise summary of the "Ong debate" (55–68).

3. Kaufer and Carley (1993) call this feature "reach"; I discuss it in Chapter 2.

4. Ong notes that these features help describe the differences between spoken and written discourse. For example, oral communication (such as stories) aggregates and builds on itself, often repeating information (redundancy), because listeners cannot refer back to a written text. Oral communication can also be agonistic in ways that written communication cannot (through body language or vocal inflection). Welch (1999, 184–186) and others have used these features to analyze electronic text. The literature on Ong is far too extensive to cover here; see Welch 1999 or Ong 1988 for more details.

5. The review of Western literacy in this section is just one version: my version.

6. I thank John Logie for reminding me of this when I asked him why he thought that the number-one ecommerce site, Amazon.com, happens to sell hard-copy books.

7. This research includes, e.g., Bolter 1991; Landow 1992; Heim 1999; and Selfe 1990.

8. Thanks to Jack Selzer for reminding me that that Darwin himself did not associate evolution with progress, yet ever since Darwin we have invoked his name in this fashion.

9. Even biological organisms don't always evolve apart from human intervention. Humans have been selectively breeding plants and animals for thousands of years and, some would argue, continue to do so via genetic engineering.

10. Similarly, Carolyn Miller (1978) has called this "technological consciousness."

CHAPTER 2: SPEED, REACH, ANONYMITY, INTERACTIVITY

1. Alone, these features are also evident in print (see Kaufer and Carley 1993), television, and other media. But the combination of these features makes cyberspace unique.
2. It is clearly problematic when icons reflecting one set of cultural standards are imposed on the world at large.
3. Katie was never found, but in August 2000, after a long investigation, a Minnesota man was found guilty of her kidnapping and murder after evidence (including a burned tooth and human bones) was found in a fire pit on his land. During the investigation, and especially during the emotional trial and sentencing hearing, people continued to post supportive comments to the Web site.
4. Naturally, the issue is a bit more complex. Authors of printed texts have played with identity switching for years, and even in face-to-face settings, people experiment with identity and gender switching. In this section, I point out the unique ways such manipulation takes place on the Internet.
5. See www.interesting-people.org/199804/0073.html for more information on the case of www.pokey.org.

CHAPTER 4: GENDER(S) AND VIRTUALITIES

1. I have removed the author's last name to save him any potential embarrassment. (Elsewhere in this chapter I have also used initials only.) Obviously, such discourse was part of the culture at that time.
2. I should note that *Wired* itself has some work to do: from reading the bylines, it appears that most of the journalists are male. Plus, with a quick glance at *Wired*, particularly its early issues, one gets a sense of gender bias in its images and stories.

CHAPTER 6: PRIVACY AND COPYRIGHT IN DIGITAL SPACE

1. Zuboff describes computer workers in the 1980s, when information technology was first making its way into many companies. These em-

ployees could be "watched" via the computer terminal, because supervisors could tell if they stopped typing or got up for a break. Zuboff compares this situation to Jeremy Bentham's concept of the panopticon: a prison designed with one-way mirrors where prisoners never know if they are being watched. The idea is also used by philosopher Michel Foucault to describe similar situations in prisons.

2. I would have preferred to cite the Forrester study itself, but when I tried to read it on the Forrester Web site, I was asked to fill out a form applying for "guest" status. This form required that I fill in my name and email address, and I chose not to do this.

3. See David Flaherty (1989) for the most comprehensive work on European models for data protection.

4. For more information on copyright in the electronic forum, see Cavazos and Morin 1994 and Gurak 1996. There is also a wealth of information available on the Web, including the Library of Congress's Copyright Office page (lcweb.loc.gov/copyright/resces.html), the Intellectual Property Mall at Franklin Pierce Law Center (www.ipmall.fplc.edu), and the CNI Copyright Forum (www.cni.org/Hforums/cni-copyright).

5. The White Paper on Intellectual Property and the National Information Infrastructure was released to explain this legislation and is available at www.uspto.gov/web/offices/com/doc/ipnii/index.html. Pamela Samuelson's excellent critique of this paper is also available online; see Samuelson 1996.

REFERENCES

Agre, Phil. 1998. RRE notes and recommendations. *Red Rock Eater News Service*. Retrieved 15 December 1999 from the World Wide Web: http://rre@lists.gseis.ucla.edu

Amazon.com. 2000. Your privacy. Retrieved 1 October 1999 from the World Wide Web: http://www.amazon.com/exec/obidos/subst/misc/policy/privacy.html/002-7358561-9666649

Anderson, Rachel. 1999. Native Americans and the digital divide. *Communications policy and practice* (Benton Foundation). Retrieved 16 November 1999 from the World Wide Web: http://www.benton.org/DigitalBeat/db101499.html

Annenberg Public Policy Center, University of Pennsylvania. 1999. National survey shows parents are deeply fearful about the Internet's influence on their children. Retrieved 19 September 2000 from the World Wide Web: http://appcpenn.org/internet/

Arbitron Pathfinder Study. 1999. PC home ownership doubles while home usage stagnates reveals pathfinder study. Retrieved 9 January 2000 from the World Wide Web: http://internet.arbitron.com/mainfiles/pcownership.htm

Aristotle. 1991. *On rhetoric: A theory of civic discourse*. Trans. George A. Kennedy. New York: Oxford University Press.

Bambury, Paul. 1998. A taxonomy of Internet commerce. *First Monday* 3 (10). Retrieved 5 October 1999 from the World Wide Web: http://firstmonday.dk/issues/issue3_10/bambury/index.html

Bermant, C. 1999. Two-way talk discouraged on web sites. *Minneapolis Star-Tribune* (originally from Newhouse News), 21 March.

Bolter, J. David. 1991. *Writing space: The computer, hypertext, and the history of writing*. Mahwah, N.J.: Erlbaum.

Bouman, Ole. 1996. *Realspace in quicktimes: Architecture and digitization*. Rotterdam, Netherlands: Nai Publishers.

Brock, Bernard L. 1989. The dramatistic approach. In Bernard L. Brock, Robert L. Scott, and James W. Chesebro (Eds.), *Methods of rhetorical criticism: A twentieth-century perspective* (183–195). Detroit: Wayne State University Press.

Brock, Bernard L., Robert L. Scott, and James W. Chesebro. 1989. An introduction to rhetorical criticism. In Bernard L. Brock, Robert L. Scott, and James W. Chesebro (Eds.), *Methods of rhetorical criticism: A twentieth-century perspective* (10–22). Detroit: Wayne State University Press.

Brown, Janelle. 1996. Girl gamers: Sugar, spice, everything profitable? *Wired news.* Retrieved 19 November 1999 from the World Wide Web: http://www.wired.com/news/culture/0,1284,516,00.html

Burke, Kenneth. 1973. *The philosophy of literary form: Studies in symbolic action.* 3rd ed. Berkeley: University of California Press.

Cavazos, Edward A., and Gavino Morin. 1994. *Cyberspace and the law: Your rights and duties in the on-line world.* Cambridge: MIT Press.

Center for On-Line Addiction. 1999. What is Internet addiction? Retrieved 15 September 2000 from the World Wide Web: http://www.netaddiction.com/whatis.htm

Clausing, Jeri. 1999. Intel alters plan said to undermine PC users' privacy. *New York Times,* 2 January.

Concord Communications. 1999. Network rage survey results. Retrieved 12 November 1999 from the World Wide Web: http://www.concord.com/library/network_rage/

Cox, Beth. 2000. Internet news.com study: Online consumers willing to pay more for food. Retrieved 17 January 1999 from the World Wide Web: http://www.internetnews.com/ec-news/article/0,1087,4_284611,00.html

Cranor, Lorrie Faith, and Brian A. LaMacchia. 1998. Spam! *Communications of the ACM* 41 (8): 74–83. Retrieved 19 September 2000 from the World Wide Web: http://www.acm.org/pubs/citations/journals/cacm/1998-41-8/p74-cranor/

Dibble, Julian. 1993. A rape in cyberspace. *Village Voice,* December 21. Retrieved 19 September 2000 from the World Wide Web: http://www.levity.com/julian/bungle.html or http://www.levity.com/julian/bungle_vv.html

Doheny-Farina, Stephen. 1996. *The wired neighborhood.* New Haven: Yale University Press.

Drudge, Matt. 1998. Anyone with a modem can report on the world. Retrieved 2 June 1999 from the World Wide Web: http://www.frontpagemag.com/archives/miscellaneous/drudge.htm

Dyson, Freeman J. 1999. *The Sun, the genome, and the Internet: Tools of scientific revolutions.* Oxford: Oxford University Press.

Eisenstein, Elizabeth. 1993. *The printing revolution in early modern Europe.*

(Canto Series). Abridged. Cambridge: Cambridge University Press, April.

Electronic Frontier Foundation. 1999. Flame, blather and spew. Retrieved 3 December 1999 from the World Wide Web: http://www.eff.org/papers/eegtti/eeg_78.html

Electronic Privacy Information Center (EPIC). 1999a. Surfer beware, III: Privacy policies without privacy protection. Retrieved December 1999 from the World Wide Web: http://www.epic.org/reports/surfer-beware3.html

———. 1999b. Study of 100 shopping sites. Executive Summary. Retrieved 18 September 2000 from the World Wide Web: http://www.epic.org

Emery, David. 2000. Current net hoaxes, urban legends, and other digital lies. . . . Retrieved 3 January 2000 from the World Wide Web: http://urbanlegends.about.com/culture/urbanlegends/library/blhoax.htm

EPIC Alert. 1999. TRUSTe fails to launch investigation into RealNetworks. Volume 6.19. November 11. Retrieved 9 January 2001 from the World Wide Web: http://www.epic.org/alert/EPIC_Alert_6.19.html

Etzioni, Amitai. 1999. Privacy isn't dead yet. *New York Times,* 6 April.

F-Secure Corporation. 2000. Hoax warnings. Retrieved 3 January 2000 from the World Wide Web: http://www.europe.datafellows.com/virus-info/hoax/

Faigley, Lester. 1992. *Fragments of rationality: Postmodernity and the subject of composition.* Pittsburgh: University of Pittsburgh Press.

———. 1999. Material literacy and visual design. In Jack Selzer and Sharon Crowley (Eds.), *Rhetorical Bodies* (171–201). Madison: University of Wisconsin Press.

Flaherty, David H. 1989. *Protecting privacy in surveillance societies.* Chapel Hill: University of North Carolina Press.

Foss, Sonja K. 1989. *Rhetorical criticism: Exploration and practice.* Prospect Heights, Ill.: Waveland Press.

Friedman, Thomas L. 1999. The Y2K social disease. *New York Times,* 10 August.

Gardner, Janet. 1999. Does your access have a gender? Getting and keeping women on line. Paper presented at the 2nd Biennial Feminism(s) and Rhetoric(s) Conference, University of Minnesota, Minneapolis.

Gilster, Paul. 1997. *Digital literacy.* New York: Wiley.

Gray, John. 1992. *Men are from Mars, women are from Venus: A practical guide for improving communication and getting what you want in your relationships.* New York: HarperCollins.

Gurak, Laura J. 1996. The multifaceted and novel nature of using cyber-texts as research data. In Teresa M. Harrison and Timothy Stephen (Eds.), *Computer networking and scholarly communication in the twenty-first-century university* (151–165). Albany, N.Y.: State University of New York Press.

———. 1997. *Persuasion and privacy in cyberspace: The online protests over Lotus MarketPlace and the Clipper Chip.* New Haven: Yale University Press.

Haas, Christina. 1996. *Writing technology: Studies on the materiality of literacy.* Mahwah, N.J.: Erlbaum.

Haraway, Donna. 1997. *Modest-Witness@Second-Millennium.FemaleMan-Meets-OncoMouse: Feminisma and technoscience.* New York: Routledge.

Harbrecht, Doug. 1998. Opening remarks for Matt Drudge at the National Press Club. Retrieved 2 June 1999 from the World Wide Web: http://www.frontpagemag.com/archives/miscellaneous/drudge.htm

Harmon, Amy. 1999. With the best research and intentions, a game maker fails. *New York Times,* 22 March.

Heim, Michael. 1999. *Electric language: A philosophical study of word processing.* 2nd ed. New Haven: Yale University Press.

Herring, Susan. 1993. Gender and democracy in computer-mediated communication. *Electronic Journal of Communication* 3 (2): 1–12.

Hirsch, E. D., Jr. 1988. *Cultural literacy: What every American needs to know.* New York: Vintage.

Hornig, Lilli S. 1989. Women in technology. *Technology Review* 92: 29–40.

IBM. 2000. Think leadership: Privacy in play. Retrieved 11 July 1999 from the World Wide Web: http://www.ibm.com/thinkmag/articles/privacy/privacy.html

Kaplan, Carl S. 2000. Judge says recording of electronic chats is legal. *New York Times,* 14 January. Retrieved 19 September 2000 from the World Wide Web: http://www.nytimes.com/library/tech/00/01/cyber/cyberlaw/14law.html

Katsh, M. Ethan. 1995. *Law in a digital world.* New York: Oxford University Press.

Kaufer, David S., and Kathleen M. Carley. 1993. *Communication at a distance: The influence of print on sociocultural organization and change.* Hillsdale, N.J.: Erlbaum.

Kidder, Tracy. 1981. *The soul of a new machine.* New York: Avon.

Kirkman, Catherine. 1996. Copyright: Alive and well in the digital age. *Web techniques* (May): 14–17.

Kraut, R., M. Patterson, V. Lundmark, S. Kiesler, T. Mukophadhyay, and W. Scherlis. 1998. Internet paradox: A social technology that reduces social involvement and psychological well-being? *American Psychologist* 53 (9): 1017–1031. Retrieved 19 September 2000 from the World Wide Web: http://www.apa.org/journals/amp/amp5391017.html

Landow, George P. 1992. *Hypertext: The convergence of contemporary critical theory and technology.* Baltimore: Johns Hopkins University Press.

Laurel, Brenda. 2000. Home Page. Retrieved 20 April 1999 from the World Wide Web: http://www.tauzero.com/Brenda_Laurel/

Lea, M., T. O'Shea, P. Fung, and R. Spears (1992). "Flaming" in computer-mediated communication: Observations, explanations, implications. In M. Lea (Ed.), *Contexts of computer-mediated communication* (89–112). London: Harvester Wheatsheaf.

Lessig, Lawrence. 1999. *Code and other laws of cyberspace.* New York: Basic Books.

Levinson, Paul. 1999. *Digital McLuhan: A guide to the information millennium.* New York: Routledge.

Lewis, Peter H. 1994. An ad (gasp!) in cyberspace. *New York Times,* 19 April.

Licklider, J. R. C., R. W. Taylor, and E. Herbert. 1968. The computer as a communication device. *Science and Technology* (April): 21–31.

Literacy Volunteers of America. 1999. About LVA and literacy. Retrieved 16 November 1999 from the World Wide Web: http://www.literacyvolunteers.org/about/index.htm

Logie, John. 1999. Toss your cookies. Paper presented at the Modern Language Association annual conference, Chicago.

Lohr, Steve. 1999. Microsoft starts the recruiting for its next war. *New York Times,* 9 September.

MacFarquhar, N. 1999. For the first time in war, e-mail plays a vital role. *New York Times,* 29 March.

Markoff, John. 2000. Security flaw discovered at online bank: Easy electronic transfers of money nationwide were allowed. *New York Times,* 28 January. Retrieved 19 September 2000 from the World Wide Web: http://www.nytimes.com/library/tech/00/01/biztech/articles/28secure.html

Marriot, Michel. 1999. Rising tide: Sites born of hate. *New York Times,* 18 March.

Martin, Chuck. 1999. *Net future: The seven cybertrends that will drive your business, create new wealth, and define your future.* New York: McGraw-Hill.

Mendels, Pamela. 1999. Offensive e-mail at Stanford. *New York Times,* 9 June.

Miller, Carolyn R. 1978. Technology as a form of consciousness: A study of contemporary ethos. *Central States Speech Journal* 29: 228–236.

Mitchell, William J. 1995. *City of bits: Space, place, and the infobahn.* Cambridge: MIT Press.

Murray, Janet. 1997. *Hamlet on the holodeck: The future of narrative in cyberspace.* Cambridge: MIT Press.

Newsweek. 1999. Special report on e-life. 20 September.

Noble, David F. 1986. *Forces of production: A social history of industrial automation.* New York: Oxford University Press.

———. 1992. *A world without women: The Christian clerical culture of western science.* New York: Oxford University Press.

———. 1999. Digital diploma mills, part IV: Rehearsal for the revolution. *Red Rock Eater News Service (RRE),* November. Retrieved 26 November 1999 from the World Wide Web: http://dlis.gseis.ucla.edu/people/pagre/rre.html

Okerson, Ann. 1996. Who owns digital works? *Scientific American* 275 (1): 80–84.

Ong, Walter J. 1988. *Orality and literacy: The technologizing of the word.* London: Routledge.

Pacey, Arnold. 1985. *The culture of technology.* Cambridge: MIT Press.

Patry, William F. 1985. *The fair use privilege in copyright law.* Washington, D.C.: Bureau of National Affairs.

Patterson, L. Ray, and Stanley W. Lindberg. 1991. *The nature of copyright: A law of users' rights.* Athens, Ga.: University of Georgia Press.

People for Internet Responsibility (PFIR). (1999). Why was PFIR formed? Retrieved 24 November 1999 from the World Wide Web: http://www.pfir.org/

Pew Research Center for the People and the Press. 1998. Online newcomers more middle-brow, less work-oriented: The Internet news audience goes ordinary. Retrieved 14 January 1999 from the World Wide Web: http://www.people-press.org/tech98sum.htm

Rheingold, Howard. 1993. *The virtual community: Homesteading on the electronic frontier.* Reading, Mass.: Addison-Wesley.

Samuelson, Pamela. 1996. The copyright grab. Retrieved 15 September 2000 from the World Wide Web: http://www.wired.com/wired/archive/4.01/white.paper_pr.html

Selfe, Cynthia L. 1990. Computers in English departments: The rhetoric of techno/power. In Deborah H. Holdstein and Cynthia L. Selfe (Eds.), *Computers and writing: Theory, research, practice* 95–103. New York: Modern Language Association.

Shea, Virginia. 1999. Nettiquette. Retrieved 10 November 1999 from the World Wide Web: http://www.albion.com/netiquette/corerules.html

Shirky, Clay. 2000. It's for real. Quoted. Retrieved 3 January 1999 from the World Wide Web: http://www.datafellows.fi/vl-faq.htm#A7

Slatalla, Michelle. 1999. The office meeting that never ends. *New York Times,* 23 September.

Stalder, Felix. 1999. Beyond portals and gifts: Towards a bottom-up net-economy. *First Monday* 4 (1). Retrieved 4 January 1999 from the World Wide Web: http://firstmonday.dk/issues/issue4_1/stalder/index.html

Standage, Tom. 1998. *The Victorian Internet.* New York: Berkeley Books.

Starke-Meyerring, Doreen, and Kirk St.Amant. 1999. Directing digital dataflows: The EU data privacy directive and American communication practices. Internet Studies Center, University of Minnesota. Retrieved 19 September 2000 from the World Wide Web: http://www.isc.umn.edu/research/internlcomm.htm

Stone, Allucquere Rosanne. 1992. Will the real body please stand up? Boundary stories about virtual cultures. In Michael Benedikt (Ed.), *Cyberspace: First steps* (81–118). Cambridge: MIT Press.

Street, Brian V. 1984. *Literacy in theory and practice.* Cambridge: Cambridge University Press.

Tannen, Deborah. 1991. *You just don't understand: Women and men in conversation.* New York: Ballentine.

Turkle, Sherry. 1995. *Life on the screen: Identity in the age of the Internet.* New York: Simon and Schuster.

Turkle, Sherry, and Seymour Papert. 1990. Epistemological pluralism: Styles and voices within the computer culture. *Signs* 16 (1): 128–157.

Tyner, Kathleen. 1998. *Literacy in a digital world: Teaching and learning in the age of information.* Mahwah, N.J.: Erlbaum.

U.S. Commerce Department. 1998. The emerging digital economy. Retrieved 15 September 2000, from the World Wide Web: http://www.ecommerce.gov/emerging.htm

———. 1999. New commerce report shows dramatic growth in number of Americans connected to Internet. Retrieved 8 July 1999 from the World Wide Web: http://204.193.246.62/public.nsf/docs/070799-new-report-falling-through-the-net-digital-divide

Van Gelder, Lindsay. 1990. The strange case of the electronic lover. In
Gary Gumpert and Sandra L. Fish (Eds.), *Talking to strangers: Mediated
therapeutic communication* (128–142). Norwood, N.J.: Ablex.

Warnick, Barbara. 1999. Masculinizing the feminine: Inviting women
online ca. 1997. *Critical Studies in Mass Communication* 16 (1): 1–19.

Welch, Kathleen E. 1999. *Electric rhetoric: Classical rhetoric, oralism, and a new
literacy.* Cambridge: MIT Press.

Woodmansee, Martha, and Peter Jaszi. (1995). The law of texts: Copyright
in the academy. *College English* 57 (7): 769–787.

Young, Kimberly. 2000. *Caught in the net: How to recognize the signs of Internet
addiction and a winning strategy for recovery.* New York: Wiley.

Zappen, James P., Laura J. Gurak, and Stephen Doheny-Farina. 1997.
Rhetoric, community, and cyberspace. *Rhetoric review* 15 (2): 400–419.
Retrieved 19 September 2000 from the World Wide Web:
http://www.rpi.edu/~zappenj/Publications/Texts/rhetoric.html

Zuboff, Shoshana. 1988. *In the age of the smart machine.* New York: Basic
Books.

SITES FOR CYBERLITERACY

The sites listed below provide more information on the topics discussed in each chapter. Web sites can disappear without warning; for updated links, check out the Web companion to this book at www.cyberliteracy.net. In the following descriptions of Web sites, information in quotation marks is taken directly from the cited page.

CHAPTER 1: CYBERLITERACY

People for Internet Responsibility
www.pfir.org/

"PFIR is a global, grassroots, ad hoc network of individuals who are concerned about the current and future operations, development, management, and regulation of the Internet in responsible manners. The goal of PFIR is to help provide a resource for individuals around the world to gain an ability to help impact these crucial Internet issues, which will affect virtually all aspects of our cultures, societies, and lives in the 21st century. PFIR is non-partisan, has no political agenda, and does not engage in lobbying."

Computer Professionals for Social Responsibility
www.cpsr.org/

"CPSR is a public-interest alliance of computer scientists and others concerned about the impact of computer technology on society. We work to influence decisions regarding the development and use of computers because those decisions have far-reaching consequences and reflect our basic values and priorities."

Electronic Frontier Foundation
www.eff.org/

"EFF, the Electronic Frontier Foundation, is a non-profit, non-partisan organization working in the public interest to protect fundamental civil liberties, including privacy and freedom of expression, in the arena of computers and the Internet."

The Internet Society

www.isoc.org/

"The Internet Society is a non-profit, non-governmental, international, professional membership organization. It focuses on: standards, education, and policy issues. Its more than 150 organization and 8,600 individual members in over 170 nations worldwide represent a veritable who's who of the Internet community."

Red Rock Eater News

dlis.gseis.ucla.edu/people/pagre/rre.html

"The Red Rock Eater News Service (RRE) is a mailing list organized by Phil Agre. . . . Subscribers to the list receive five or ten messages a week on average. These messages have no single format; they simply contain whatever I find interesting. These days most of the messages tend to concern the social and political aspects of computing and networking."

The Berkman Center for Internet & Society at Harvard Law School

cyber.law.harvard.edu/

"The Berkman Center for Internet & Society is a research program founded to explore cyberspace, share in its study, and help pioneer its development. The Center is a network of teaching and research faculty from Harvard Law School and elsewhere—as well as students, fellows, entrepreneurs, lawyers, and virtual architects working to identify and engage the challenges and opportunities of cyberspace."

CHAPTER 2: SPEED, REACH, ANONYMITY, INTERACTIVITY

Anonymizer.com

www.anonymizer.com

"Protect your online activities from third party snooping. We provide the security and privacy tools you need to remain anonymous. The Anonymizer is more than just an anonymous proxy; it disables cookies, java and javascript and provides useful features such as URL Encryption and Safe Cookies."

U.S. Federal Trade Commission on Identity Theft

www.consumer.gov/idtheft

"How can someone steal your identity? By co-opting your name, Social Security number, credit card number, or some other piece of your personal information for their own use. In short, identity theft occurs when someone appropriates your personal information without your knowledge to commit fraud or theft." This site encourages you to visit often for the latest updates.

The Electronic Frontier Foundation's Unofficial Smiley Dictionary
www.eff.org/papers/eegtti/eeg_286.html
Email "smileys," also known as emoticons, are ways to insert oral qualities, like smiling or frowning, into an email message. "This Unofficial Smiley Dictionary is only one of many different collections by various 'editors' you'll come across at many places on the Net."

The UCLA Internet Report — "Surveying the Digital Future" by the UCLA Center for Communications Policy
www.college.ucla.edu/InternetReport/
A survey and report on the global impact of the Internet.

CHAPTER 3: TECHNO-RAGE

Silicone Valley Tarot, the Flame War Card
svtarot.com/net/flamewar.html
"Two pedants, locked in mortal combat, scorch each other with fiery words . . . "

Roadmap File: Flame War
www.df.lth.se/~df-libr/Roadmap/File.Flame_War.html
"The following flame war recently occurred on a 'relatively quiet Usenet newsgroup.'"

Flamology Theory
www.mcs.net/~jorn/html/flamers.html
A series of posts to alt.culture.usenet and news.future (August 1993) on Usenets and flaming.

The Flamers Bible
comedy.clari.net/rhf/jokes/88q1/13785.8.html
"Here, I have attempted to document the Art of Flaming, in such a way as it will be interesting to old hands (flame masters) and novices (virgins) alike." Humor.

Flame, Blather and Spew from EFF's (Extended) Guide to the Internet
www.eff.org/papers/eegtti/eeg_78.html#sec79
Describes various net.characters, including flamers and blatherers.

Netiquette 101: The Flame Form Letter
www.wap.org/ifaq/computers/flameform.html
A humorous "check the box" generic flame letter.

The Jargon Lexicon
www.tuxedo.org/~esr/jargon/html/The-Jargon-Lexicon.html
Definitions of flamage, flame, flame bait, flame on, flame war, and flamer. (Click on the letter *F* and then on the various flame topics.)

Flame Response
www.wap.org/ifaq/computers/flameresponse.html

Anti-Defamation League
www.adl.org
A classic response to a flame.

CHAPTER 4: GENDER(S) AND VIRTUALITIES

Computer Professionals for Social Responsibility (CPSR)
www.cpsr.org/publications/newsletters/issues/2000/Winter2000/
This site is the Winter 2000 issue of the *CPSR Newsletter* (18, no. 1). "The purpose of this newsletter is to explore how the Internet and other computing advances subvert or reinforce gender roles."

Voices of Girls in Science, Mathematics, and Technology
www.ael.org/nsf/voices/
"Voices is a three-year project to help girls do well and feel confident in science, math, and technology. Girls are as capable as boys, but do not participate as fully as boys do in these subjects."

Communication Studies: Gender and Race in Media
www.uiowa.edu/~commstud/resources/GenderMedia/cyber.html
Gender- and race-related links from the University of Iowa Department of Communication Studies.

FeMiNa

www.femina.com/

"FeMiNa was created in September of 1995 and debuted online to provide women with a comprehensive, searchable directory of links to female friendly sites and information on the World Wide Web. FeMiNa is the only website of its kind, with a comprehensive database and powerful, intuitive search engine created by Cybergrrl, Inc." It includes a page of best sites that has links to some exceptional sites for and about women (www.femina.com/best.html).

New Moon: A Magazine for Girls and Their Dreams

www.newmoon.org/

The Web site for New Moon: A Magazine for Girls and Their Dreams, "an international magazine for every girl who wants her voice heard and her dreams taken seriously. With girl editors ages 8 to 14 and girl contributors from all over the world, New Moon celebrates girls, explores the passage from girl to woman, and builds healthy resistance to gender inequities. The New Moon girl is true to herself, and New Moon helps her as she pursues her unique path in life, moving confidently out into the world."

Brillo

www.virago-net.com/brillo/

Described by Virginia Eubanks (www.cpsr.org/publications/newsletters/issues/2000/Winter2000/eubanks.html) as "an electronic journal devoted to the inclusion of marginalized voices in the movement towards a global information infrastructure. It's also cranky and witty and feminist and funny."

CHAPTER 5: HUMOR, HOAXES, AND LEGENDS

Urban Legends

urbanlegends.about.com/culture/urbanlegends/

Excellent urban legends archive from about.com, with a search engine to help you find a specific legend. (More generally, about.com is a great resource: "The network of sites led by expert guides.")

The AFU and Urban Legends Archive

www.urbanlegends.com

This site, associated with the Usenet newsgroup alt.folklore.urban (AFU), contains legends organized by topic and has a search engine.

Yahoo! Urban Legends site

dir.yahoo.com / Society_and_Culture / Mythology_and_Folklore /
Urban_Legends /

Provides links to verify urban legends.

Don't Spread That Hoax!

www.nonprofit.net / hoax /

Provides links to verify urban legends and hoaxes.

Computer Viruses and Hoaxes page by the Computer Incident Advisory Capability

ciac.llnl.gov / ciac /

This site, provided as a public service, is a reliable source of information about computer viruses.

F-Secure Corporation's Computer Virus Info Center

www.datafellows.com / virus-info /

"This service is provided by the F-Secure Anti-Virus Support Team. The database is updated several times a week. The virus description service was started on the 13th of June, 1994. Now in its fifth year, this site was the first anti-virus web site ever — and is considered the industry standard source for up-to-date information on new viruses and hoax alerts."

The Texas Network Site

www.texasnetwork.com / virus.html

"This page provides links to verify virus or email hoaxes."

Yahoo! Urban Legends Site: Computer Viruses

dir.yahoo.com / Society_and_Culture / Mythology_and_Folklore /
Urban_Legends / Computer_Viruses /

Provides links to verify computer virus hoaxes.

Virus Bulletin

www.virusbtn.com /

"The international publication on computer virus prevention, recognition, and removal."

Symantec Antivirus Research Center (SARC)

www.symantec.com / avcenter /

"SARC is committed to providing swift, global responses to computer virus threats, proactively researching and developing technologies that eliminate such threats and educating the public on safe computing practices."

McAffee Virus Information Library
vil.mcafee.com/
"McAfee.com, in partnership with AVERT, a division of NAI Labs, tracks emerging PC virus threats constantly. . . . In addition to genuine viruses, the Virus Information Library contains a useful database on virus hoaxes, those dire email warnings about disk-eating attachments that sometimes land in your inbox."

VirusBuster
www.vbuster.hu
A Hungarian site on hoaxes.

Web Searching
dir.yahoo.com/Computers_and_Internet/Internet/World_Wide_Web/ Searching_the_Web/
A Yahoo site on searching the Web.

Online! A Reference Guide to Using Internet Sources
www.bedfordstmartins.com/online/
An online guide to using Internet sources, by Andrew Harnack and Eugene Kleppinger.

CHAPTER 6: PRIVACY AND COPYRIGHT
IN DIGITAL SPACE

Electronic Privacy Information Center
www.epic.org/
"EPIC is a public interest research center in Washington, D.C. It was established in 1994 to focus public attention on emerging civil liberties issues and to protect privacy, the First Amendment, and constitutional values."

The Privacy Forum
www.vortex.com/privacy
"The PRIVACY Forum, created in 1992 by Lauren Weinstein, includes a moderated e-mail digest . . . for the discussion and analysis of issues relating to privacy (both personal and collective) in the information age. Topics in-

clude telecommunications, information and database collection and sharing, and a wide range of other privacy issues, as pertains to the privacy concerns of individuals, groups, businesses, government, and society at large."

Privacy Place

www.privacyplace.com/

"The online magazine that concerns itself exclusively with issues of personal privacy."

EFF's Top 12 Ways to Protect Your Online Privacy

www.eff.org/pub/Privacy/eff_privacy_top_12.html

This site, written by EFF Advocacy Director Stanton McCandlish, identifies twelve things you can do (such as turning off cookies or examining privacy policies) to take control of your personal information online.

Junkbusters

www.junkbusters.com/

"The Mission of JUNKBUSTERS . . . is to free the world from junk communications. We give you the tools to stop junk. Our web site is one of the world's most comprehensive collections of information about junk messages and how to stop them. We want everyone to know how to enforce their 'right to be let alone.' We also alert you about threats to your privacy from direct marketers. The Internet Junkbuster helps you control commercial communications to your web browser. We also give you new ways to use your browser to control other kinds of junk." Other sites on blocking Web banner advertisements and cookies include www.ecst.csuchico.edu/~atman/spam/adblock.html, www.precipice.org/privacy/, and opt-out.cdt.org/.

Journal of Computer-Mediated Communication, Special Issue on Law on the Electronic Frontier

www.ascusc.org/jcmc/vol2/issue2/

Articles about copyright, privacy, consumer protection, and more.

U.S. Copyright Office

lcweb.loc.gov/copyright/

Copyright information, from the basics to the complex.

The Copyright Website

www.benedict.com/contents.htm

Copyright basics, news, and specifics about the visual, digital, and audio arts.

EFF "Intellectual Property Online: Patent, Trademark, Copyright" Archive
www.eff.org/pub/Intellectual_property/
Many links to intellectual property resources.

Copyright and Fair Use
fairuse.stanford.edu/
Provides links to information on fair use.

10 Big Myths about Copyright Explained
www.templetons.com/brad/copymyths.html
"An attempt to answer common myths about copyright seen on the net and cover issues related to copyright and USENET/Internet publication."

CHAPTER 7: SHOPPING AT THE E-MALL

Consumer Reports Guide to Online Shopping
www.consumerreports.org/Special/Samples/Reports/9812shpo.htm
"Shopping by computer may be the biggest change in the way consumers make purchases since the advent of the department store 100 years ago. This guide will help first-time cybershoppers navigate through unfamiliar territory, find their best value, and avoid snags when buying online."

U.S. Department of Commerce, *The Emerging Digital Economy*
www.ecommerce.gov/emerging.htm
"The Emerging Digital Economy report represents an initial step by the Clinton Administration and the U.S. Department of Commerce to better understand the effect of electronic commerce on the economy. The report presents both economic analysis and case studies that paint a picture of the importance of electronic commerce and information technologies to the economy as a whole and to individual sectors of the economy."

CMPNet Primer on Shopping Online
www.netguide.com/special/primers/shopping/start.html
A CMPNet NetGuide introduction to online shopping.

Consumer World
www.consumerworld.org/
This site is a "public service, non-commercial guide cataloging over 2000 of the most useful consumer resources" and offers many links, including warnings of online shopping scams.

Shopping Tips: Playing the Price Is Right, The Internet Edition

www.gomez.com/features/article.cfm?topcat_id=0&col=70&id=4113

Discusses various online shopping methodologies and some benefits and drawbacks of each.

Gomez.com — The Ecommerce Authority

www.gomez.com/

"Gomez Advisors provides decision support to consumers that want to transact online and information to businesses that want to attract and retain online consumers."

CHAPTER 8: THINK GLOBALLY, EAT LOCALLY

SETI at Home Project

setiathome.ssl.berkeley.edu/

"SETI@home is a scientific experiment that uses Internet-connected computers in the Search for Extraterrestrial Intelligence (SETI). You can participate by running a free program that downloads and analyzes radio telescope data."

Twin Cities Free-Net: Helping Communities Help Themselves through Internet Technologies

freenet.msp.mn.us/

"TCFN is a nonprofit organization that promotes community through electronic communication for all. We've been linking the people of Minneapolis, St. Paul and neighboring communities since 1995." This site provides links to neighborhood and other community resources, as well as inexpensive email and Web pages for residents of the Twin Cities metropolitan area. Most cities have easily locatable Freenets.

Psych Central's Internet Addiction Guide

www.psychcentral.com/netaddiction/

Defines and describes Internet addiction and provides links to other useful resources.

City of Bits

mitpress.mit.edu/e-books/City_of_Bits/

"The City of Bits Web site is an imaginative, compelling, and dynamic companion to the 'analog' book by William J. Mitchell, dean of the School of Architecture and Planning at MIT."

NASA

www.nasa.gov/

The NASA site, with its images from space, reminds us that we live on the earth, not in cyberspace.

Page numbers in italics refer to illustrations.

other sources, 104–6; language on, 2, 13, 21; mainstream concerns about, 6–7, 10–11; pre-Web, 9, 45; shooting incident at startup firm, 1; and shopping, 1–2 (*see also* ecommerce); social spaces changed by, 3–4, 9–10, 21, 66; and the theory of evolution, 24–25, 163n.8

Internet addiction, 152, 153–154, *153*

Internet fatigue, 151–152

Internet2, 143

Intervale Research Company, 75

Japan, 121

Jaszi, Peter, 7, 125

JavaNet, 145–146

Jeep Web site, 134, *134*, 135, 155

"Joan," 39, 80, 149

jokes, 83, 90–91

Karjala, Dennis, 7

"Katie," 37, 164n.3

Katsh, M. Ethan, 124

Kaufer, David, 17, 34

Kidder, Tracy, 96

Kirkman, Catherine, 123

Kroninger, Stephen, *139*

laissez-faire, 136; and the Internet, 25, 26; and privacy legislation, 116, 117, 119, 126

LambdaMOO, 148

language: blend of oral and written, 2, 13, 21, 22, 51; and icons, 36, 164n.2; and speed of communication online, 30–32

Laurel, Brenda, 75

Lea, Martin, 50

Lefevre, Karen, 7

Lessig, Lawrence, 61, 63, 126

Levinson, Paul, 20, 48

Lewinsky, Monica, 105

Life on the Screen (Turkle), 39, 152

lifestyle enclaves, 37

Lindberg, Stanley W., 125

literacy: and all discourse, 13, 163n.1; and communication technology, 21; conventions from older technologies, 16; defined, 9, 12–13, 21, 22; digital, 27; electronic, 21–22, 26–27; history of Western, 17–18, 163n.5; as performance, 13, 22, 27; and power, 21–22

Literacy in a Digital World (Tyner), 12

Literacy Volunteers of America, 22–23

Logie, John, 7, 114, 126, 163n.6

logotypes, 35

Lotus Development Corporation, 106

Lotus MarketPlace, 3, 34, 37, 73, 106, 113

Lunsford, Andrea, 7

Lynx, 45

Mall of America, 135–136

Mankato, Minn., 92, 93, *93*, 94

Martin, Chuck, 128, 138

Mattel, 75, 77

Mayo Clinic, 90, *90*

MCI, 65, 66

McLuhan, Marshall, 20, 34, 48

"meat space," 155

media, 164n.1

Microsoft Corporation, 24, 75

Microsoft Word, 18